5|10|12
$19.95
I

AS

the American MUSTANG Guidebook

Wild bachelor stallions at home in Nightingale Mountain Herd Management Area (HMA) in Nevada. Strawberry roans, such as the horse in the center, are common here.

the American MUSTANG Guidebook

History, Behavior, and State-by-State Directions on Where to Best View America's Wild Horses

BY LISA DINES

Willow Creek® PRESS

© 2001 Lisa Dines

Published by Willow Creek Press, P.O. Box 147, Minocqua, Wisconsin 54548

Design by Pat Linder
Edited by Andrea Donner

For information on other Willow Creek Press titles, call 1-800-850-9453

Library of Congress Cataloging-in-Publication Data
Dines, Lisa
The American mustang guidebook : history, behavior & state-by-state directions on
where to best view America's wild horses / Lisa Dines
p. cm.
ISBN 1-57223-403-2 (softcover : alk. paper)
1. Mustang. 2. Wild horses—United States. 3. Wild horse watching—United States—
Guidebooks. 4. United States—Guidebooks. I. Title.
SF293.M9 D56 2001
599.665'5'0973--dc21
00-012791

Printed in the United States of America

To Kate and Joel—my favorite
mustang-watching partners,
and Clippy, Lalo, Clay, Blitzen, and
Cirrus, the mustangs who have
taught us so much.
—L.D.

Beautiful, gentled, halter-trained grey and red chestnut geldings await adoption in Burns, Oregon.

Contents

Introduction

During my forays through the United States in search of herds of mustangs to enjoy, I began to dream of writing a guidebook that would include everything I had wanted to know but couldn't find (all in one place) before I set out.

I began this project by reading as many books as possible that have been written about American mustangs, and gazing at all the pictures I could find of the beautiful horses that roam wild in the U.S. I am grateful for all these authors and photographers who have lived with, studied, and delved deeply into the history of wild horses in America. I have learned a great deal from the variety of works published, which range from archived, long-out-of-print, non-fiction texts on original Spanish Horses, to fictional or poetically-accompanied modern photographic essays on wild horses found on coffee tables—mine included.

A portion of my interest in this subject was the desire to adopt a BLM mustang, and an obsessive interest in knowing *everything* about these horses. (For many of us, this "horse fever" accompanies owning *any* equine, and it's not easily explained!)

In the process of adopting a wild horse, and in researching this book, I entered a previously-unknown world of people and animals with problems and joys I had never imagined. I spoke to BLM (Bureau of Land Management) employees who expressed the frustration of trying to protect wild horses while still adhering to public grazing rights. I met a group of extremely dedicated volunteers who saved a small herd of wild horses with asymptomatic EIA (Equine Infectious Anemia), and who still feed and care for them every day, and keep them safely quarantined on donated land at their own expense. On a daily basis, I keep in contact with members of a wild horse internet list who are going through adopting, gentling, training—and "explaining"—their mustangs to those unfamiliar with the breed. The more I became interested in mustangs, the more doors opened up to visiting the "wild ones." I rode in a fishing boat to Shackleford Island, NC, and was given a guided tour of the "Banker Ponies" (including being told all their names) by one of their devoted caretakers. A Jeep was my next vehicle into wild horse country where I got to watch an exciting gather, and help sort horses courtesy of the Bureau of Land Management in Nevada. In Colorado, I rode horseback on domesticated mustangs and, led by a local mustang fan, was given a tour of the Little Bookcliffs Wild Horse Range, including a quick cross-country detour to avoid the band of wild horses crossing the road in front of us. And with a topographical map, lunch, binoculars, invaluable advice from the BLM and local mustang-loving citizens, and my trusty pickup (with spare tires AND the tools for changing them), I spent many pleasant hours "treasure-hunting" for bands of wild horses in Nevada, Oregon, New Mexico, and California (all the while dreaming about Wyoming, Utah, Montana, Idaho, and all the herds I hadn't seen yet). I was able to locate central watering holes and regular grazing sites, and stumble across breathtaking bands of wild horses that looked like sparkling jewels against a backdrop of sand and rock.

During this time, I also visited Palomino Valley Holding Facility near Sparks, Nevada. I spent several hot, summer days on the outsides of two immense corrals (300 wild horses in each one) observing and scribbling down necktag numbers during the wild horse hunt for a mustang of my own to adopt. This introduction would not be complete without a few words about "Clippy" (short for "Sahwave's Eclipse"—named for the Sahwave Mountains in Nevada, and the large white moon on his dark forehead), the first mustang I adopted from the BLM in September, 1998.

This young horse is so different from the domestic, well-trained, Thoroughbred-cross I had when I was a teenager. We are far closer, this sturdy survivor from the steep sagebrush valleys, this small, hook-eared purple roan, and I. He has changed forever my ability to "fall asleep at the reins" down the familiar paths of trail riding and basic gaits, yet his calm acceptance of trailering, veterinary and farrier visits is impressive. Riding and being around Clippy has taught me much about basic horse behavior. For instance, I now know why my domestic mare liked to overlook scenic vistas. I know not because of Clippy's serene enjoyment, but from my small gelding's *insistence* that we get out of the creekbed, up the side of the hill, to the top of the mesa above the trees—NOW! From a higher vista, once-wild Clippy alertly scans the horizon for wild horses, grass, and the direction he deems best. In fact, if he could talk, I'm sure

Top: "Slash," one of Shackleford Island's tiny stallions. Above: Sargeant Howard Mason riding "Sgt. Skye," a mustang police horse, in Vallejo. (Also see Skye at http://hometown.aol.com/)

Wild mares and foals are reflected in a lake at The Wild Horse Sanctuary near Shingletown, California.

he would tell me how he survived a vulnerable colthood, worked his way up in a competitive herd, then led the other young bachelors to food. If he could talk, we would also have some interesting debates about who is qualified to lead whom! As strong-minded as Clippy is, he is also openly affectionate toward humans, and willing to do what is asked. The smallest at 13 hands, and the eldest horse at six years, Clippy is now ridden by 12-year-old Molly. Although he will never again know the freedom of the Nevada desert, and never sire friendly, strong-minded little baby roans, he was one of the 1,000 excess mustangs that had to be gathered that summer to prevent overcrowding and starvation. Even though I know he would enjoy "smelling the sagebrush" for fun and adventure, I am absolutely sure he would return to us at feeding time, for grooming and safety.

There are many mustangs in holding pens, at adoptions, in the classified sections of newspapers, and on the internet waiting for permanent, loving owners who will treasure them. Sometimes wild horses are mis-

Above: Flaxen, chestnut-colored mustang named "Snort" and his owner demonstrate polo-cross.

Left: One of the original "Stone Cabin Grey" wild stallions gathered in Nevada. Due to the loss of grazing rights on the public land he has roamed for more than 20 years, this majestic old-timer and others like him that are considered unadoptable will probably live out their remaining years in a BLM holding corral or sanctuary.

Introduction

BLM mustangs comfort each other with closeness during a New Mexico adoption. Opposite page: Two of Shackleford Island, North Carolina's year-round beachfront residents, Picasso (front) and Julius.

understood, mishandled, or mistaken for targets by misguided humans, but in far greater numbers I have found that American Mustangs are well-cared-for family members, competing show horses, working mounts, trained pleasure horses, and strong survivors of a start in life that might have killed a different breed.

This book is an invitation for you to enter this adventurous wild horse world, to enjoy your public lands with wild horses running free, to get to know the folks who protect, train, and promote mustangs, and maybe to adopt one of your own. With this book as a guide, you can educate yourself on their history, habits, and locations and, with respect and delight, visit the wild ones yourself! Wild horses are good for the soul, have been domesticated to serve us as our helpmates for most of recorded history, and may need your help now to continue to run free.

Introduction

The History of the American Mustang

The horse as a species originated in North America, but prehistoric horses died out here thousands of years ago. No one is exactly certain why all the horses vanished from this continent. Other large land mammals, such as the saber-toothed tiger, mastodon, and woolly mammoth also became extinct at the same time.

After the horses vanished, huge herds of bison and antelope continued to flourish on the abundantly grassy plains where they had grazed beside the horses. Some say disease, others point to a change in climate from dust clouds after a meteor's impact, and still others say that being hunted to extinction by early man is the most probable cause of the horses complete disappearance from North America. Whatever the reason, no fossil remains of the horse have been found in North America dating past 7000 BC, and when the first European explorers came to the Americas in 1500 AD, the native people of that time had never seen horses.

Luckily, horses lived to reproduce in Europe and Asia after crossing the land bridge that existed between the two continents during prehistoric times. Three of the many (long-extinct) early horses were the Polish Forest horse, a massive, probably dapple-coated, draft-type horse with large hooves for walking over boggy ground; the Siberian Tundra horse, a small, thick-coated white pony; and the Oriental horse, small and graceful with possibly a dished face.

For many thousands of years, horses were eaten—not ridden. Cave paintings found in France from the Later Stone Age (about 40,000 to 8,000 BC) show horses (with short black legs, black tails, and upright black manes) pierced with arrows. During the New Stone Age (from about 6,000 to 3,500 BC) people began to grow crops such as wheat and barley instead of gathering wild plants, and raised animals such as pigs, sheep, and goats for food rather than following the wild herds from place to place. They constructed stone or mudbrick houses, but still considered the horse only a large game animal.

Chestnut and bay-colored mustang mares with "Stone Cabin Grey" stallion, at a waterhole near Tonopah, Nevada.

Finally, artwork shows horses pulling wheeled chariots containing soldiers or hunters in the Early Dynastic Period (around 2700 BC). From approximately 500 BC, Greek pottery depicts bareback riders with bridled steeds, and chariots pulled by horses participating in funeral processions, games, and races. In approximately 450 BC, the Athenian general and horseman, Xenophon, wrote *The Art of Horsemanship* (a natural horse handling classic which is still read today!). When the Parthenon was constructed in Athens in 400 BC, carvings made in the marble walls show adept horsemen riding bareback with no bridles. A larger-than-life-size bronze statue of Roman emperor Marcus Aurelius riding a tall, powerful warhorse wearing a saddle and bridle was erected in 165 AD. In 800 to 1000 AD, medieval Europeans sheltered both themselves and their horses in the same wooden barns.

The horse had at last become an important partner and friend to man, far too useful just to eat. From then on, horses were selectively bred for qualities such as size, speed, and appearance. By the 1500s, horse breeds such as Arabs and Barbs were created in the Middle East and Africa, and the larger Andalusian warhorse was bred in Spain. From 1600 to 1800, a combination of these types, known simply as the "Spanish Horse" or the "jennet," was popular all across Europe.

Genetically different than earlier horses is the "Przewalski's Horse," which roamed Mongolia. A small, dun-colored, ass-like animal with a heavy jaw and head, dorsal stripe, black legs (sometimes with zebra stripes), black tail and upright black mane, it was hunted to extinction in the wild, but a number were preserved and bred in captivity in the early 1900s. Przewalski's Horses can be seen in some zoos today, and successful efforts have now been made to reintroduce them back to their native Asian Steppe homelands.

Horses finally "returned" to the Americas when the Spanish explored and started to settle North America in the 1500s. They established breeding ranches in the Southwest territories from 1600 to 1700. The Spanish horses that escaped, were turned loose, or stolen established feral herds that became quite large in North America. A wild horse was called a "mesteno" or "mestango," which was Anglicized to "mustang."

Today, most American Mustangs are the result of breeding between the original, faster, leaner, "hotter" jennets, and larger, calmer, draft breeds such as the Percheron, Belgian, Clydesdale, or larger, more refined Thoroughbred and carriage horses introduced over the years by ranchers, farmers, and the U.S. cavalry. Still existing today are just a few isolated "purer" herds which were not crossed with those of settlers or the cavalry. When genetically tested, they prove to have more "original Spanish" DNA and less resemblance to introduced breeds.

Due to the large expanse of grasslands, horses successfully fit back into the ecosystem in North America. Early American settlers deliberately added domestic stallions and mares to free-roaming herds to "improve" the size or quality (from which the settlers could capture new youngsters later), and settlers' domestic horses joined mustang herds after being freed by raids or destruction. For all of these reasons, by the 1860s, *two million mustangs* covered the plains of the United States. The largest wild-horse range of all was in Texas where grazing herds reportedly stretched for twenty miles at a time.

Despite this abundance, however, few people were interested in capturing and taming wild horses. They were considered difficult to catch and troublesome to train. Pure mustangs were thought by settlers and ranchers to be too small for plowing, cattle roping, or driving. The

Newly gelded, these adopted mustangs await pickup at Palomino Valley Holding Facility in Sparks, Nevada. Unusual colors shown are: (left) chestnut rabicano, (second from left) apricot dun, strawberry roan (in front), and dark brown overo (right).

Native American tribes had already traded or stolen enough horses from the Spanish to be well-equipped by the end of the 1700s. For all of these reasons, huge herds of mustangs continued to graze unhindered in many western states. In the early 1900s, even more horses were added to the mustang herds when farmers and ranchers abandoned them during the Great Depression, and as the demand for horses was greatly reduced due to the invention of the automobile and tractor.

Eventually, Texas reduced its "problem" wild horse population by constructing rendering plants and turning most of its mustangs into fertilizer or pet food. Wild horses were shot in the legs or eyes to cripple them, or run to exhaustion with planes or trucks, tightly packed into trucks, and taken to slaughterhouses where the only requirement was that they still be barely alive at the time of sale.

In the early 1900s ranchers and farmers all over the U.S. began fencing in their livestock with newly-invented barbed wire, which fenced many herds away from sources of food and water, and prevented them from outdistancing winter snowstorms. In addition, mustangs were shipped overseas to aid war efforts, and shot for competing with domestic livestock for grass and water.

In 1959, a woman named Velma Johnson (nicknamed "Wild Horse Annie") watched a truckload of suffering and bleeding mustangs being

Chestnut-colored, flaxen-maned "Darcy" anticipates the arrival of her 1999 foal on Shackleford Island, North Carolina.

delivered to a slaughterhouse and decided to spearhead legislation to deny permits to chase down and shoot mustangs from motorized vehicles. From her home in Nevada, she began a major, nationwide campaign (that included schoolchildren from all across America) writing letters to government officials protesting the killing of American Mustangs.

In 1971, Congress passed a bill protecting "wild free-roaming horses and burros." The management and protection of these "living symbols of the historic and pioneer spirit of the West" was turned over to the U.S. Department of the Interior's Bureau of Land Management (BLM), or in a few states, the U.S. Forest Service. (Unfortunately, wild horses on state, reservation, or U.S. Park Service lands today are not protected by this Act.)

Since then, the BLM, primarily, has had the difficult job of deciding how many horses can be sustained on the millions of public grazing acres called Herd Management Areas (HMAs) located in ten western states. Other large herbivores such as deer, elk, pronghorn antelope, bighorn sheep, and domestic beef cattle coexist there, as do numerous plants, birds, mammals, insects, reptiles, fish and other living species, and the ecosystem must be managed to allow all to survive.

Today, because of their protected status, great adaptability and suitability to the environment, and because they have few natural enemies (usually only man, drought, fire, and the mountain lion), mustang populations have grown in the U.S. Today, there are approximately 42,000 mustangs roaming 186 HMAs in ten western states. Nevada contains 23,214, Wyoming 6,279, California 3,700, Utah 4,380, Oregon 2,536, Colorado 755, Idaho 813, New Mexico 55, Montana 176, and Arizona 205. Additonal wild horses are on lands not governed by the BLM in North Carolina, Louisiana, Georgia, Maryland/Virginia stateline, North Dakota, Missouri, South Dakota, and Hawaii, which brings the total wild horse population in the U.S. to around 50,000. More than half the population roams Nevada's desolate desert and mountains.

Unfortunately there exists human territorial competition over public lands in this country that involves wild horses directly. Cattle growers pay for feed and space for their cattle on public land, hunters pay to shoot game on public lands, natural resources can be extracted at a cost to companies, and there are sightseers, campers and photographers who don't benefit monetarily but whose taxes help support the lands they enjoy. As is common in human interactions, "the squeaking wheel gets the grease" and lobbyists for any side in federal courts can try to supersede their

This Shackleford Island resident looks much like the primitive Exmoor Pony from the coast of England.

interests on federal lands, sue for exclusive rights, or argue their cases and win in Washington D.C. far from the realities of the actual sagebrush they're fighting over.

There is debate over whether wild horses are really native to the areas (where they first evolved prehistorically) or to other areas in the U.S. where they have lived for hundreds of years after being placed there by man. Disagreement over the term "wild" versus "feral" is ongoing. Should horses as wild as deer whose ancestors hundreds of years ago were feral still be called feral, and why? The reason for much of the semantic argument is for protection based on classification. If a species is "non-native," or "feral" it can be argued that it deserves no protection. Henceforth, it can be eradicated. Why would anyone want to eradicate wild horses or wild burros? Because they compete for the same feed and water as other creatures, and the humans managing the land decide who uses the land. Therefore, all people must educate themselves as to how their lands should be used. Can abuses occur in huge governmental bodies comprised of humans with individual interests and beliefs — sure. Unless land disappears there will always be people fighting over it. Some of the questions you will hear are: will the wild horses be "zeroed out" or completely gathered from many HMAs on public land unfairly without citizens' knowledge; are the counts of horse populations accurate or skewed higher for removal purposes; is the land really over-grazed or waterholes damaged by wild horses or are cattle more destructive; why aren't cattle removed when the range is poor; and many more issues that are complex, and impossible to determine without careful research. People should ask questions and find the answers for the benefit of the public lands. Learn as much as you can about the BLM and how they manage the land, the Forest Service, the Park Service, and the wild horses and burros and other species that live on our public lands. Help make educated decisions that will affect everyone.

Under BLM management, when wild horses exceed the number allowed inside an HMA , or stray outside its boundaries, the BLM holds a "gather," using slow-moving helicopters and riders on horseback. Mustangs are herded into corral traps, then transferred to a sorting area by truck and separated into age and gender groups. They are then trucked to a holding facility where they are inspected, given shots and wormed by a veterinarian, and freeze-branded with a permanent neck brand. Horses over ten years old are usually taken to a sanctuary holding facility. Horses from five to nine years of age are often transferred to contracted trainers (stallions are gelded first) or programs such as prison programs to be gentled and trained.

The rest of the horses are kept in the holding facility to be viewed by the public and adopted. Some are transferred to adoptions elsewhere, or photographed for internet adoptions.

To adopt a mustang, one must go through an approval process with the BLM's "Adopt a Horse or Burro" program. Those requesting information will be given the requirements for shelter, corral size and other paperwork to be filled out and submitted to the BLM. (See "Your Very Own Mustang" chapter for more details on adopting.)

The future of the American Mustang will probably include population control. Over the next five years, the BLM wants to reduce the wild horse population to about 27,000. (They also hope to increase adoptions from approximately 7,000 a year to at least 10,000 a year.) Mares can be injected with a vaccine that makes them unable to conceive. This vaccine is reversible, non-damaging to foals the mares might be carrying, does not affect the environment, and allows the herds to continue to display breeding behavior. Tests are being done on stallion birth control methods as well. The stress of gathering and injecting mustangs is an adverse factor in population control, however.

Mustangs should be enjoyed, protected and adopted! Unfortunately, some people steal or kill horses or destroy BLM horse facilities. If you observe anyone harming or harassing horses (or other wildlife, plantlife or facilities), *immediately* notify the BLM, law enforcement, or animal rescue groups in the area. Stopping these harmful activities ensures enjoyment for future generations—human *and* horse.

Mustang watching is *not* confined only to the western U.S. This book will tell you how to find and enjoy feral horses in parks, on islands, and in sanctuaries in many other states too. Enjoy!

Wild Mustang Behavior

Wild horses prefer to graze on flat, grassy plains where they can see in all directions — and that's where you can see them best as well. During your travels through rugged, isolated Western states or in other U.S. wild horse areas, you might spot horses grazing in large unfenced fields, meadows, or hillsides. If they are not anywhere near ranches or homes, they may be wild horses—especially in Nevada.

Generally speaking, how horses watch *you* is most important in deciding whether they are wild or domestic. Tame horses pay attention only when you are very close, may approach you in a friendly manner, or perhaps walk or trot away slowly. Mustangs, on the other hand, will raise their heads, point their ears, and tense their bodies from a great distance away. If you do not try to approach mustangs too closely, you can observe them fairly easily. If you violate their safety zone, they will let you know with body language. A good rule is that if they move away, you should stop moving closer.

High-powered binoculars are very helpful for mustang watching, as are telephoto lenses for photographing them. Of particular importance when approaching wild horses is a "non-predatory" stance. Horses are prey animals with eyes on the sides of their heads to better see while grazing, with long, strong legs for quick flight, and ears and nostrils that can detect you long before you see them. If you walk visibly and directly toward a herd of horses, they will run. If you meander slowly and innocently, first this way, then that way in a sideways approach, keeping your eyes averted, they will perceive you as far less threatening. If you sit down to watch from a comfortable distance away, the horses will probably stop and stare at you curiously.

Herds accustomed to friendly human visitors will allow closer viewing. Herds on some military ranges, in popular wild horse refuges, or

Typical family group — a watchful stallion stands guard over mare and foal on Shackleford Island, North Carolina.

those that have had regular, positive interactions with humans can become quite bold. One herd in Death Valley Junction, California, walks across the highway at its own "Horse Crossing" sign to be regularly fed and watered by a local citizen! Mustangs are backyard visitors, like deer, in some residential areas near wild horse ranges near Carson City, Nevada. One Bishop, California, herd tolerates constant human contact in a mountain casino parking lot during foaling season to stay safe from predatory mountain lions. Wild burros are daily visitors to the streets of Oatman, Arizona.

To see *most* mustangs, however, you will probably have to look off the beaten path. To detect the presence of mustangs while driving or hiking through their ranges, watch for "stud piles" (large mounds of manure to which each visiting stallion adds his "calling card" on top).

In the winter, mustangs will come to lower elevations to graze. Mustangs can eat snow for water, and thus conserve energy by not traveling to and from the water hole during cold weather. They will paw snow to uncover grass in the lowlands, or travel to steep mountainsides where grass is uncovered naturally by the blowing winds.

If you approach wild horses in a meandering way with your eyes on the ground, they will often let you get quite close, as these beautiful pintos did on South Steens Mountain in Oregon.

During the summer (when most herd management area dirt roads are passable), wild horses find the temperatures cooler and the grass more plentiful in higher, more mountainous areas. Wild horses must water at least once a day during the summer, and herds can often be located at a water source early or late in the day. Unless disturbed, wild horses usually confine their daily travels to a four-mile radius of their water hole, dictated by the location of grass.

Mustangs live in family groups consisting of (but not led by) one dominant breeding stallion (usually five years of age or older), one to 12 breeding mares, their nursing foals (birth to one year old), and weaned colts (males) and fillies (females). Colts reaching sexual maturity (at about age three) are driven from the herd by the dominant stallion, especially during the spring breeding season. Fillies at or prior to their first heat are usually driven out or leave the herd, and are then gathered up into another herd by another stallion. In this way, related animals have less chance of breeding with one another, unless the total herd number is too small. The absolute minimum viable population size is said by genetics experts to be 50 horses, but a population of 100 or more is recommended. Inbreeding is detected by a larger number of individuals with genetic defects such as very small size, cataracts, and white coat color.

"Bachelor bands" (herds of stallions) or lone bachelors are commonly seen on mustang ranges. Some stallions are content to take a subordinate, non-breeding position in order to remain within the safety of the herd. Mares most often travel within a herd, but have been observed occasionally living alone or with a few other mares.

A combination of age, length of time in the herd and on the range (wisdom), size and temperament determine who will be the highest-ranking mares or stallions. Herds are led by an experienced, trusted older mare with the dominant stallion bringing up the rear, biting at herd members to keep them moving. Stallions take on a protective role also, and have been known to prevent herd members from drinking at a water hole before thoroughly investigating it for predators or man. Horses drink in order of rank. Stallions will stand watch over the herd while grabbing quick mouthfuls of grass. Wild horses will trade "sentinel" duty to be alert for approaching danger.

If you surprise a family of mustangs in the wild, the stallion will probably stand his ground. Stallions have been known to bite or kick humans to protect their mares and foals, but most of the time will wait until the rest of the herd is safe, and then they, too, will whirl and disappear.

Fearful wild horses will snort to take in your scent, toss their heads to see you better, and prance and stamp their feet in anticipation of running. Wild horses exhibiting this "flight or fight" behavior can be quite exciting to watch and photograph, but this is very stressful on the horses, especially during foaling time. For this reason (and the condition of roads in winter and spring), it is better to wait until summer or fall to view wild horses. And of course, never deliberately scare or chase horses just to see them run any time of the year.

Breeding season for wild mustangs is spring to early summer. During this time you can see courtship and affection between stallions and mares as they prepare for mating. Often a mare will have a very young foal at her side when she goes into a "foal heat." This ensures that no interruptions occur in the production of young. Wild mares can be quite prolific during their lifetimes, beginning to bear one foal every year as early as when they are two years old. Often, mares will still produce offspring until their twenties. Wild horse herds can experience a 15 percent or higher growth rate each year.

Young stallions fight for dominance during breeding season on Shackleford Island, North Carolina.

During breeding season, a stallion will aggressively prevent his mares from leaving the herd by "driving them" back in when they stray. This behavior is demonstrated by laying his ears back and twisting his head and neck in a "snaking" motion toward any mares or foals that stray. Herd members learn quickly to respect this posturing, and rarely need the painful bite that accompanies it.

Stallions often carry visible injuries and scars from fighting off other dominant stallions. When a herd stallion is displaced by losing a fight to another male, he will usually roam alone or with a bachelor band.

Mares have an 11-month gestation period. Most wild mustang foals are born in April, May, or early June. Some are seen as early as February or as late as September. Foals born in the middle of spring have the most time to grow strong before the cold weather comes again. A mare nurses her new foal during the spring, summer, and first winter after its birth, and weans it just before giving birth to the next one. If she has no new foal, a mare may continue to nurse her offspring until it is quite large.

Watching the play and exploration of colts and fillies is entertaining. Often they will engage in mock battles as they rear up and drop down quickly to try to bite the legs or bellies of their playmates. They chase each other in exuberance, pivoting quickly on their hind legs and rearing

Top: A colorful wild herd near Dulce, New Mexico, contains from left: dappled grulla, white, grey, black, sabino, palomino, and chestnut horses.
Above: Free-roaming Native American horses add to the beauty of this northern Arizona landscape.

Buckskin-colored mare and foal in Death Valley Junction, California.

slightly as they stop and change direction. (This natural chasing and pivoting behavior of horses has been utilized by man to chase and hunt game, or to herd cattle.)

Horses can live until their forties or older, but most have life spans of up to 30 years. Still active and robust, wild horses are gathered off the ranges and aged at "20+" if conditions have been favorable. Disease and injuries occur in wild horse herd, although some animals are able to overcome adversity and recover, or remain in the herd with a disfiguring condition. Wild horses have been known to manage with a clubfoot or even blindness, depending on the rest of the herd for safety and direction.

Although mustang family groups' overall ranges may overlap, each band waters and feeds at separate times to avoid conflict. When you see many bands running together (such as during a gather) you are seeing the forced combination of bands that would normally stay apart. When these neighboring bands are trapped together in initial holding pens, there is much danger and fighting as stallions continue to "guard" their mares from one another. The BLM staff will quickly separate horses by age and gender to prevent injuries. Once stallions are separated into

Opposite page: Dominant horses drink first, and then so on down the pecking order at a waterhole on Shackleford Island.

bachelor herds away from mares, their fighting loses its intensity and purpose. A surprisingly large number of stallions can coexist rather peacefully together in large holding facility corrals.

Over time, and without man's interference, nature selects horses with certain qualities best suited to survival in the wild. Horses will become leaner, smaller, possess stronger bones, teeth, and hooves, have less noticeable color, and a more alert, cautious nature. However, since a larger, calmer, taller horse with flashy white markings is more desirable to humans, most mustang herds have had draft, carriage, riding or working horse stallions introduced to "improve" the horses for future gathers.

Black mustang "chooses" a human to bond with at Palomino Valley Holding Facility in Nevada.

Mustang enthusiasts treasure the few remaining herds that have not been directly "produced" by people. These herds still contain horses which show predominately "original Spanish" characteristics with little resemblance to introduced stock. These horses are said to be more "Spanish" in appearance and "hotter" in blood (more alert). However, there is debate as to what constitutes a "Spanish-type" mustang. The original "pure Spanish" horse from which mustangs descended was actually a mixture of Arab, Barb and Andalusian known as the "jennet," which no longer exists in Spain today (although the Sorraia horse is still bred in Portugal). Some believe that the most "Spanish-type" mustang is a Sorraia-type mustang, with narrow sides, "rafter" hips, and a convex profile. Some registries allow BLM mustangs regardless of type, while others prefer a certain conformation.

The influence of generations of introduced sires has produced a wide variety of types and temperaments today. Draft horse background has produced larger bones, feathered legs, "colder" or calmer temperaments,

Telltale sign of a wild horse track: no shoes, and a hoof naturally kept so short that the V-shaped "frog" contacts the earth.

and certain color patterns such as sabino and roan. Thoroughbred horses used as Cavalry mounts show their influence in herds of dark horses with little or no white (harder for an enemy to detect) that are also taller with long legs and bodies. You will also see herds of appaloosa colors, pintos, horses with Friesian ancestry, palominos, strawberry roans, and mahogany bays that look like polished teakwood.

An easy way to see a vast variety of mustangs of all different colors and types is to visit a BLM holding facility. They are located in a half dozen states across the U.S. (the largest is Palomino Valley Holding Facility, located near Sparks, NV). You can also attend a local BLM adoption, or annual Mustang and Burro Show. If you want to see wild horses in their natural settings, this book will help you find them. If you are respectful of their needs and behaviors, you can spend many enjoyable hours learning firsthand about horse behavior from the truest teacher on the range — the American Mustang.

Important Safety Guidelines for Wild Horse Watching

When traveling, or camping in primitive, public wild horse areas, please remember:

- Call and visit the BLM Office in that district for topographical maps and additional information on road conditions and gathers *before* you arrive.

- Use vehicles in good working condition appropriate for rough terrain, such as high-clearance four-wheel drives, with spare tires, *tools to change them*, and plenty of fuel.

- Bring plenty of water and food.

- Stay on approved roads, and camp only in designated areas.

A confident mustang foal crosses at its own road sign in Death Valley Junction, California.

- Keep track of the weather.

- Stay off military installation grounds.

- Don't park or camp near water holes. Visit them early or late in the day, and then leave.

- Pack out all garbage, and observe fire regulations.

- Leave all gates as you find them.

- Never try to touch or feed wild horses.

- Keep dogs quiet and leashed; do not allow them to chase or scare horses.

- Keep noxious plant seeds off the ranges. Don't bring them in on clothing or in vehicles.

- *Bring plenty of film and camera batteries!*

Wild mustang filly finds people just as interesting as they find her in Death Valley Junction.

Your Very Own Mustang or Burro

In addition to watching wild mustangs and burros, you can actually own one if you meet the BLM qualifications. You must have a certain amount of well-fenced land, a shelter, and the ability to care for a horse or burro properly. Adoption applications are on the BLM websites, or can be obtained at adoption facilities and in BLM office locations listed throughout this book.

Gentling and training wild mustangs and burros provides an unequaled opportunity to bond with and understand the equine species in their purest form. If you think that you are going to be able to do this cheaply, however, remember that the adoption fee is the least expensive part of the whole experience! A $75 burro or $125 mustang will cost you plenty by the time he or she is properly transported home, gentled, gelded, fed, trained, vetted, and groomed. However, the initial cost is a very enticing feature of the BLM program.

Unfortunately, some people adopt thinking that the low price means the process of gentling is easy (or even unnecessary), and that they have just bought their children a new toy or themselves a weekend project. The biggest problem facing wild horses and burros is new adopter ignorance. For this reason, you should prepare yourself in advance before adopting. If this means you do not attend any irresistible BLM adoptions until you are totally prepared, so be it. A mustang or burro should not be an "impulse purchase" if their gentling and training are to be done properly. You will be glad you waited!

Proper Housing

The proper housing at first will consist of a strong, smaller enclosure made of BLM-approved materials. (These fencing materials may cost more than the animal!) Safe fencing for an adult wild horse can be temporary, heavy-duty 6'-high metal horse panels, either chained or "pinned" together in a square or circular shape to the diameter the BLM

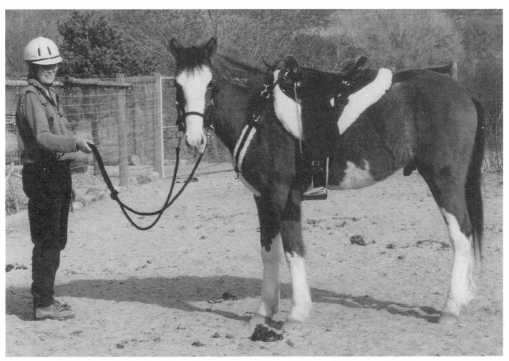

Kate proudly displays "Lalo" her bay sabino mustang from Sahwave Mountain HMA in Nevada.

specifies, or another type of approved corral fencing that is permanent, such as wooden or metal pole fencing. Metal panels are available from farm supply stores or manufacturers. There are many brands. Some are lightweight and bend rather easily; others are heavy-duty and will withstand much pressure. For a mature wild horse, the heavy-duty panels are a must. Panels come in varying lengths and are very useful for long-term needs. They can be formed into a multitude of enclosures, chutes, grazing areas, and even set up in horse camps for overnight enclosures. Other types of fencing must be set in concrete, and can include non-climb horse fencing. Metal T-posts may not be acceptable as fence posts. Check with the BLM.

A gentling pen for a wild horse needs to be big enough to give the animal a safe feeling. If the enclosure is too small, a horse may panic and try to climb over the top, run blindly into the fence, or kick and bite in defense. If the space is too large, the horse will easily avoid contact with you. A 40' round-pen is a good size. A 24' x 24' square pen should also

"Pard," a beautiful, gentled red chestnut mustang awaits adoption in Burns, Oregon.

work. Check on your local BLM requirements. You may be visited by a BLM compliance officer after filling out application forms. If you are not truthful on your application as to your enclosure, or if your housing is unsafe, you will not be allowed to adopt.

Horses like to lie down and roll. The corral should allow a horse plenty of space to do this without running into a metal panel, or getting a leg or head underneath. A shelter needs to be built over or adjoining the corral. The gate should always be as tall as the rest of the enclosure. If the horse senses a weak or low spot, he or she may try to escape over it. You can block off the opening to the shelter when training your horse, and open it again when you leave. Take all feed and water containers out of the enclosure when you are training. Make sure there are no sharp edges, nails, wires, splinters, or anything to hurt either you or the horse

The high bid for the Kiger Mustang filly in the center was $19,000 at a 1999 Burns, Oregon, adoption auction, but most animals are adopted at or near the minimum price.

as you brush against it. Horses will "test" enclosures by leaning on them and by putting their heads over them. Make sure yours can stand up to this!

Get Plenty of Advice

If this is a new experience for you, get plenty of advice *before* adopting or trying any wild horse handling on your own! Many mustangs are adopted, and their training abandoned just because the adopters failed to educate themselves. Watch videos, read books, join a mustang club or an internet list of wild horse and burro owners, talk to trainers and mustang owners who have successfully gentled and trained mustangs—you will find lots of folks out there to help you if you look.

You might find prejudice against mustangs among stable owners, vets, farriers, horse breeders, or the general horse crowd in your area. Some may try to discourage you from adopting, or tell you that mustangs are untrainable. Often these opinions are based on ignorance, or on the behavior of animals that were never gentled or trained.

When talking to trainers, realize that mustang prejudice may exist. Do not hire a trainer who expresses prejudice against an animal based on breed alone. An experienced trainer worthy of taking on a mustang will know that all horses are possessed of varying levels of "preservation instinct" due to age and life experience, and that no horse is ever "bad," just more or less afraid. Mustangs over the age of 10 are not usually adopted out by the BLM due to a higher level of fear that is hard to extinguish. Unless you have trained a horse before, it is not wise to begin your career with a wild horse; although novices have been successful at it. If you are new to adopting, it may be easier to begin with a weanling or yearling rather than a mature animal, or a gentled horse rather than one that is completely wild. Have the BLM geld a male horse before you adopt. Whatever your choice, if you learn from the right sources and pay close attention to your horse, you should succeed.

This book contains suggestions for reading material and trainers whose teachings are appropriate for a wild horse. Many trainers will not have proper facilities for handling a totally wild horse. Your job as an adopter is to make sure the horse is gentled enough to be handled and led at halter so that the horse will be able to exist in the confines of a typical barn environment should you want it to be professionally trained.

Adopting from a Bureau of Land Management (BLM) Holding Facility

After approval, and gathering information, you now have several adoption options. You may want to adopt a mustang directly from a BLM holding facility. This is where wild horses are kept after being gathered off the range. Here you will not have to attend an auction and bid against others, so you will pay the minimum amount of $75 for a burro, and $125 for a horse, or $250 if you adopt a mare and a foal as a pair. There are BLM holding facilities located in California, Colorado, Kansas, Nebraska, Nevada, Oklahoma, Oregon, Tennessee, and Utah. Adopt at a facility close to your home whenever possible. Remember, if your corral is in Florida, and the horse of your dreams is in Oregon, *you* will have to make the transportation arrangements. This means unloading the horse every 24 hours for a five-hour rest stop, at *approved BLM facilities* along the way. If you hire a professional hauler, they must be familiar with transporting wild horses, and must abide by BLM rules.

A holding facility offers the largest selection of wild horses, and the best opportunity to watch your horse move freely and interact with other horses. Although some of the horses have been there longer, none of them have been handled, except for veterinary purposes. Because the horses have had no experience with humans, they have a "clean slate" (which is better than bad habits or resentment from being poorly handled).

Holding facilities usually have no specific hours for viewing the horses, but in general, to ask about individual horses and to adopt, you must make an appointment. Spend a lot of time looking, asking questions, and giving a lot of thought to the decision before your actual adoption. Taking more time to choose will mean you *and* your horse will be happier in the long run.

Use binoculars to study the horses from outside the corrals at the holding facility to find ones that exhibit good conformation and good health. Record the tag numbers of the ones that most interest you.

Although many mustangs exhibit rare and unusual colors and markings, don't choose a horse on color alone if you intend to have a horse you can enjoy. You may notice that the gorgeous palomino with the long, sweeping mane and tail picks on the other horses in the pen nonstop, or that the flashy bay yearling with the perfect blaze and four matching socks means you won't be in the saddle for a couple of years. You may decide that the "plain-colored" horse you didn't even notice at first—the four-year-old red chestnut with large, kind eyes, good health, and sound conformation, who gets along peacefully with the others—may be your best choice.

When you meet with the BLM representative for your scheduled appointment, they will answer your questions, tell you what they know about the horses, and take you into the pens to see your final choice(s) more closely.

If you adopt a stallion, you should have him gelded at the holding facility (usually at no extra cost). Even though this means you will have to leave him there an additional period of time, there are some excellent reasons why you shouldn't take home a stallion. Geldings are much easier to handle for the average horse owner, the BLM has better facilities and veterinarians who are more experienced in gelding wild horses, and since there are more mustangs (and mustang crossbreeds) than there are good homes for them, adopting a stallion to breed and produce more is not really necessary.

"Riddler," a grullo-colored Kiger Mustang weanling feels most comfortable making contact when his trainer sits on the ground!

Traveling Adoptions

To allow people in different areas to adopt, the BLM transports a limited number of wild horses from the holding facilities to public adoptions in other cities and states. These are held in fairgrounds, horse show arenas, or other facilities with horse accommodations. In addition to a number of wild horses (and burros) brought in by the BLM, local individuals and organizations might bring their trained animals to the adoption for demonstrations. Only BLM-approved adopters can bid for horses, with bidding usually starting at $125 per horse. (Many horses at public adoptions can be purchased for the minimum amount or close to it.)

Internet Adoptions

On-line adoptions are held for a select number of horses photographed at BLM holding facilities. The BLM gives a description of the color, gender, age, where and when the horse was gathered, as well as several photos of the horse showing different angles. You must be approved by the BLM and receive a bidding number before bidding on any internet horses or burros, and bidding will go on for a certain period of time before the highest bidder wins. These horses are usually chosen because of good conformation, color, and temperament, but it is always advisable to actually see a horse (or have someone knowledgeable see the horse for you) before bidding. (The color of the horse listed depends on the person who sorted it, and might differ from your own definition.) Do not bid on an internet horse, no matter how irresistible, if you have not looked into the logistics and cost of getting the horse home! (See Picking up Your Horse for the requirements.) Horses are sometimes purchased by on-line high bidders who do not pick the horse up, thus depriving someone else the opportunity of ownership who could have followed through.

Satellite TV Down-link Adoptions

The first nationally-televised adoption was held in August, 1999, with pre-taped footage of the horses and burros moving in pens located in Nevada, while the auctioneer fielded bids in Texas from locations equipped with satellite dishes. Animals could be picked up from several BLM locations by the BLM-approved high bidders. (More will surely follow.)

Prison Adoptions

Prison facilities with wild horse inmate training programs offer public adoptions of wild or gentled horses in conjunction with the BLM. The level of training varies from halter-broken to saddle-trained, depending on the program's guarantees. Some prisons may allow you to adopt a wild horse at an adoption elsewhere, and transport your horse to the prison for training. If your horse is to be *saddle trained* at a prison, it is advisable to adopt a horse no younger than three years of age whose joints are sufficiently mature to allow it to bear weight at different gaits. (A horse can be *gentled* safely at any age.) If you contract with a prison program to have your mustang trained, it can take 90 days or longer, and visiting hours will vary. For adopters living far away, this may not be an issue. If you plan on visiting your horse "in the pen," find out if security rules apply, such as getting clearance far in advance, and limited picture-taking.

Prison training should not replace bonding, gentling and training by the adopter or a professional trainer. Prison training methods are specific to that population and riding style, and a horse may need to be retrained for different purposes at a later time. Prison training is valuable for intial gentling (especially for horses from five to 10 years), allowing the adopter or trainer to continue the process in the slowest, most complete way possible. A gentled horse is much easier to load, handle and interact with, and may not require special facilities for housing when adopted. A good assessment of individual horses can also be made at the prison, and a good match between adopter and horse made.

Picking Up and Trailering

When you adopt an ungentled adult horse, the BLM will allow you to pick it up from the holding facility or adoption location *only* in a stock trailer with no drop ramp. (The specifications for taking home a gentled or trained mustang, or a weanling, yearling or a burro may differ—check with the facility.) Stock trailers have no inside partitions to injure a frightened horse, and, lacking a drop ramp, can be backed up directly to the loading chute.

The wranglers will fit a halter and lead rope on your new horse, if you like. Some people prefer to leave this off. Halters and ropes left on unattended horses have been known to snag on fences and feed troughs, causing injury and even death when the wild horse panics. A halter and a long drag rope can be used as a training tool in experienced hands.

Your mustang may be quite anxious while in the trailer—alone for the first time in its life, and in a small, confined space with cars and trucks whizzing noisily past. Once you start driving, the horse must work constantly to maintain its balance, which takes a physical and mental toll. Often, wild horses will not eat, drink, or relax while in the trailer. For these health reasons, the BLM requires you to stop, unload, and rest the horse for five hours *at a BLM-approved facility* for every 24 hours in the trailer.

Arriving Home

However, you might be surprised to discover how safe your horse has found the inside of your trailer to be when you arrive home and it does

The day you arrive home, build a continuous, strong chute or back up directly to the pen, and let your wild horse come out of the trailer when he or she feels comfortable.

not want to come out! Back up your trailer directly to the gate of your animal's pen and unload, or build a chute of tall corral panels or fencing material (leaving no gaps or weak spots a strong, frightened horse could push through or jump over) leading directly into your new mustang's pen. Open the trailer door, and allow the horse to come out calmly, smelling everything before making the next move. Never rush or scare a wild horse out by yelling or banging on the trailer—your horse may injure itself by rearing, slipping, or falling. If you associate the trailer with calmness and safety from the beginning, training your mustang to load into a trailer in the future will be much easier. Place feed and water ahead in the new pen to offer a hungry horse the incentive to move. Once in the pen, allow the horse to rest and acclimatize to its new surroundings for a couple of days before beginning training.

Placing your horse in a small gentling pen at first will give you more opportunity to get to know the horse, and vice versa. A 40-foot round-pen, or a similar-sized square pen constructed of six-foot high (BLM requirements are six feet high for adult wild horses, and five feet for yearlings and burros), heavy-duty metal horse panels (including one with a gate) can make a safe, strong, temporary small enclosure. Panels of some opaque material against the pen walls to block out distractions will help the horse to focus on you and your training methods. Placing the smaller pen inside a larger, fenced pasture (no barbed wire) will ensure the new horse will still be contained if it should escape the gentling pen. Even though your new mustang will long for the chance to run free, put it in a larger pasture only when it is completely gentled and you can approach and halter it at anytime. Placing a new horse directly into a large pasture before halter-training will allow it to easily avoid you, and any training you had in mind!

If a mustang is released for the first time into a larger corral with a fence made of horse-safe, yet "see-through" material (such as non-climb wire mesh, with no larger than two-inch squares), make the fence more visible beforehand by tying small pieces of white cloth or plastic onto it. Remove the flags after a few hours (horses may chew or eat them), or as soon as possible once the horse knows its limitations. A line of horizontal poles or planks should be placed along the top of a five-foot high wire fence for more visual strength. If your new horse is halter-trained, lead it around the interior of the fence to introduce it to the new boundaries before releasing it.

Wild mustangs are naturally wary of animals they are not familiar with—which includes most domestic animals. "Introductions" to dogs, cats, chickens, goats, geese and the rest must be made slowly and carefully. Never let dogs chase a wild horse! Serious injuries, even death to both animals, can result. Eventually, mustangs and other animals will learn to coexist together, if given plenty of time, and a strong fence to separate them if necessary.

Health and Feeding

Your mustang will probably have parasites when you first adopt it, which are a natural part of the ecosystem on the range. Worms can cause the horse to be potbellied, dull-coated, or malnourished—or your horse may show none of these signs and still be wormy. Consult the BLM records that come with your adopted animal to see when the next dose of wormer is due. Worming medication can be given to a horse in its feed before the horse is gentled enough to accept a hand-held syringe. Different worms require different wormers. Check with your veterinarian who may have you provide a manure sample to determine which worms are present. Always have a correct estimate of weight before worming—an overdose can be deadly. Horses on the range usually lack enough of certain nutrients and minerals. Adding a supplement of salt and a properly balanced ratio of calcium, phosphorus, and other vitamins and minerals will help your mustang feel satisfied, and mature correctly. Giving psyllium and probiotics, and having free access to clean water at all times can help keep a horse's digestive and elimination systems healthy and reduce colic.

An automatic watering device or float on a large rubber trough hooked up to a continual water source will provide horses with sufficient water. During the winter in cold climates, a water heater can be added to prevent icing. Keep watering containers free of algae and dirt by draining and cleaning them regularly. (If available, small "mosquito fish" or "feeder goldfish" can be added to freshwater watering troughs to prey on mosquito larva.)

Always keep the pens and pastures clean and free from debris and hazards. Avoid barbed wire for fences as it can cause injuries. Provide your animals with a shelter that is large enough to prevent crowding, and tall enough for a horse to rear without hitting the ceiling. Provide feeders that are safe and appropriate to keep hay off the ground and prevent horses from eating soil and sand with their food. Know what plants in your pasture are dangerous to horses and remove them. Feed grass hay whenever possible as it is easily digestible and cannot be overfed. Alfalfa may be too rich in protein, imbalanced in minerals, and can cause excess nervous or aggressive energy if the horse is not heavily worked.

Wild horses on the range have tough, worn-down hooves. After you adopt, your horse will need its hooves trimmed regularly, although it may not need shoes unless ridden on hard, rocky surfaces. You will probably have time to gentle your horse before calling the farrier for your horse's first hoof trim.

If your horse sustains an injury, acts abnormally, or refuses to eat or drink, consult a veterinarian if you are inexperienced with symptoms or conditions of horses. Knowledgeable friends can help, but professional advice is crucial in some circumstances. Choose a veterinarian (and a farrier) who have a positive attitude toward wild horses, preferably those who have handled them before. It is your responsibility to gentle your horse as soon as possible so your vet and farrier can safely handle the horse in case of emergency or routine needs. Sedating a wild horse to care for it before it is gentled often causes a frightening loss of control for the horse, and the impulse to fight the sedation can result in injury to horse and handler.

Gentling

It is essential to understand the nature of a wild horse before attempting to gentle one. Wild horses are best understood as prey animals who perceive human beings as predators, and we are indeed predators when compared to them. Our eyes are in front of our faces for binocular vision, we move directly ahead with purpose, and we do not rely on the safety of the herd, great strength, or the ability to run fast to survive. A horse's technique for survival is to move quickly, or if unable to move, to kick and bite. These behaviors are based on fear—they do not make a horse "bad" or "stubborn." It is the job of a successful horse gentler to allow a frightened wild horse to experience humans in a consistent, nonthreatening manner so that the horse will lose the desire to flee or fight. Horses that have been successful in the wild for a number of years may need just as many years to completely trust humans.

This transfer of emotions from fear to trust will begin when you enter the pen regularly to provide food, water, and cleanup, without attempting to touch the horse. Gradually, the wild horse, a herd animal by nature, will look to you for companionship and socialization. Spend time sitting in the pen and talking to the horse (read out loud from some horse book or novel). If you sit still and avoid direct eye contact, a wild horse will eventually become so curious about you that it will approach and sniff you cautiously. Allowing the horse to initiate the first touch is the most nonthreatening approach for a wild horse.

Sooner or later, however, you will want to initiate touch so that you can groom, halter, and otherwise handle your mustang. If you have educated yourself about different methods of "resistance-free" gentling and training, you will know that some trainers advocate using a long bamboo

Using Oregon trainer John Sharp's "bamboo pole method," this zebra-dun colored mustang weanling finally allows the back of his owner's hand to touch his shoulder after a succession of closer and closer touches with the pole. His fear remains, however, as shown by his tense posture with head up, ears back, and front inside leg ready for forward action.

pole to touch a horse for the first time; others let a halter and long lead serve as "lines of communication." Some use advance and retreat inside a roundpen, while others prefer square corners, and so on. A form of operant conditioning known as "clicker training" also works well for many wild horses.

Gentling relies on the fact that a horse will become desensitized to everyday procedures like haltering, brushing, or cleaning feet, if those actions are built through a series of related steps where the horse remains comfortable. For instance, a wild horse has a normal fear of being caught by the head, or having one foot held off the ground, so start by approaching the horse slowly, from the side, and touching or rubbing the withers or shoulder first, and when the horse relaxes with this, progress to stroking the head or legs.

Always leave the area in front of a horse clear so the horse can run forward if it needs to. Calmly approach the horse from the side, and if it runs, wait until it stops, and try again. Each time you may get a little closer. Encourage the horse to run in both directions when it avoids you, so you can approach the horse from both sides of its body. Because of the way a horse's vision and brain work together to process information, a horse needs experiences on both sides of its body to learn completely. Gradually, the wild horse will realize you intend it no harm, and will slow its pace from a run, to a trot, to a walk, and finally it will just back up or raise its head while standing still to avoid contact. The horse will resign itself to the fact that "escaping" you is just not possible if, within the confines of the small gentling pen, you wait patiently in the middle of the circle or square and let the horse move around you until it stops (usually in the same place each time), and approach again without anger or impatience. When a wild horse finally allows you to touch its nose, face, or shoulders with your hand, reward it by stepping back and allowing both of you to take a breather. The time to quit for the day is when your horse finally shows some progress (however small the amount) in standing still facing you while you approach or touch. A horse's wisdom and attention span increase with age, so you may find the older the horse, the faster it catches on. Spend at least an hour a day with your new mustang, but don't push a horse hard for many hours at a time. Give your horse periodic breaks and plenty of time alone to allow it to relax, eat, drink, and look forward to your next visit.

The time it takes to gentle a wild horse depends entirely on that individual horse. Some horses are naturally more cautious—others will trust you faster. All horses should eventually allow your touch if you are patient enough. Share your progress (daily, if you need to) with others who are experienced with mustangs. Get help if you feel frustrated or unsafe.

A lucky adopter took home this nice-looking palomino mustang mare and her attractive, dusty dun foal.

Burros are calmer and less sensitive than horses. You will be able to touch, hand-feed, and handle your wild burro more easily and quickly than a wild horse. Teaching a burro to lead requires the same tools (yacht-test tied nylon rope halter and a 20' lead-rope with no metal parts is best) as with a horse. Burros, however, are not as strong or as quick. Apply the same techniques such as rewarding your burro for the smallest attempt and they will learn quickly to give to pressure.

Desensitizing

All basic horse equipment will probably scare your adopted mustang at first. Ropes, feed bags, saddle blankets, tarps, rags, plastic bags, hoof cream, fly spray, fly masks, clippers, and buckets are just a few that can cause flight reactions. Allow the horse to touch any "scary" object first with its nose. When it's relaxed with that, rub the object gently on the horse's shoulders (allowing the horse's scent to be transferred), and let the horse sniff the object again. Repeat until the horse exhibits no fear.

Training your horse to allow haltering should be broken down into steps the horse finds comfortable. After the horse allows touch, stroke the horse on the withers, then move up to the neck and mane, and finally touch its face and top of head (poll). Once you have accustomed a horse to having your hand moving around its face and head, introduce a halter and the accompanying movements of haltering, such as putting your right arm over the horse's neck while holding the halter with your left hand by the horse's nose. Gradually you can combine all movements together and halter the horse. If worked successively, with fear extinguished at every step, your horse should accept the halter with no problem. Introduce the lead rope (and use a very long lead at first) in the same way. Let the horse sniff it, rub on the shoulder and allow another sniff, simulate the actions of attaching it to the halter over and over, and when the horse accepts it calmly, attach it. (This might take an hour, or it could take a week—every horse is different.) If your horse pulls back when he feels pressure, let him move away but follow him, keeping slack in the lead. When he is comfortable with a slack lead, put a little tension in it. Keep the tension on until he takes a step forward, and immediately give him slack in the lead as a reward. He will learn to give to pressure without feeling afraid, and will be content to follow you. (Let go completely and begin again if the horse panics.)

Body Parts

When gentling your horse and touching sensitive body parts, stay out of the "kick zone!" A horse will be touchy about certain areas of its body, such as the head, belly, legs, flanks and tail. A horse can kick backwards and sideways with lightening speed and no warning. Stay away from the hind end of a wild horse, and face the horse's shoulder where you can watch both the legs and the head simultaneously. Watch for pinned ears and body weight shifting off the "kicking leg." Use a glove on the end of a pole to touch sensitive, dangerous areas until the horse is relaxed, then use your hand cautiously, but with a firm touch. Light touches can tickle a horse, and make it think your hand is a fly that needs removing!

Work your hand down the back of each leg, and pull up on the fetlock hairs to train your horse to pick up its feet. (Some people pinch the chestnut on the leg to get the horse to raise it.) Often this lesson will be hard for a mustang to learn because of the vulnerability of standing on three legs. Go slowly and calmly. A horse that has trouble balancing can have two people work on him at a time, one at his head holding the halter and lead and steadying him if he sways, and the other person picking up the feet. Encourage your horse to pick up its own feet with a command and reward method. At first, your mustang will only be comfortable with a leg held up for a split second. Hold a foot up longer and longer each time, making sure that it's you who finally sets it down. Hold the front of the hoof rather than the ankle in your cupped hand. When your horse calmly accepts each foot being lifted and held for as long as necessary, accustom the horse to having its hooves trimmed, rasped, and shod by holding them extended out the way a farrier does, and tapping and scraping while you clean them.

When your horse or burro stands still and calmly allows you to touch it *everywhere* on its body, allows you (or your farrier or vet) to pick up *all four feet* and care for the hooves, can be *approached and haltered* at any time with minimal or no avoidance, and can be *lead willingly and calmly*, you should congratulate yourself and your horse for a gentling job well done!

Your Very
Own Mustang

Understanding Your Mustang's Body Language

A t *all* times during the gentling, handling, feeding, and training of your mustang, it is crucial to pay close attention to the horse's body language to avoid dangerous flight or fight reactions. The following illustrations will help you to determine which normal emotion your horse may be feeling.

Figure 1

Fear

Most wild horses will display fear, like the dapple-grey horse in Figure 1 that has just been gathered in Nevada. Fear is displayed by head and neck held high, ears erect, "whites" showing around unblinking, widened eyes and nostrils, legs in fast forward or reverse motion, or if that is not possible, body ready for flight. Most mustangs will display this body language continuously before they are gentled, and at various times after that when something new, unexpected, or dangerous comes up.

When a horse is being ridden and does this, it is called "spooking" or "shying,"and the fast movement backwards, forwards, or sideways away from "danger" can unseat an unprepared rider. Training a wild horse to control its normal flight reaction takes time and patience, and a rider who constantly stays alert to horse body language. A well-trained riding horse is one that has learned to overcome its fears, trust the judgment and guidance of its rider, and stay in one place even if frightened. This may take years!

Figure 2

Aggression

The wild stallion in Figure 2 is protecting his mares. The clear intent conveyed here is that a bite (a normal fight response) will follow a further approach from another stallion. Aggression is shown by ears pinned to the side of the head, neck lowered, eyes narrowed, and the horse holding his ground. A horse that pins its ears and swings its rear end or lifts a hind leg menacingly is indicating an intent to kick. "Charging" forward to protect mares or feed, with the intent to bite or strike with a foreleg is another fight response. These body postures maintain rank and file between horses in a herd, but they do not mean a horse will be fierce toward people. The same dominant wild stallion, a "curly" from Nevada, is shown on page 107 displaying a calm curiosity toward the human taking his picture.

If you adopt a wild horse that displays disrespectful or threatening behavior toward you, you may get hurt if you don't assert your role as "leader." Many trainers will advocate driving the horse forward with pressure behind and toward the hip *from a safe distance away*, such as flicking a long rope toward the horse's rear each time it turns toward you, but stopping the pressure once the horse stands still and faces you without signs of aggression. If you feel afraid of your adopted mustang or feel you are in danger, get help from a more experienced trainer. Most horses that display aggression toward humans have been abused by humans. This behavior is not common to most mustangs right off the range.

Figure 3

Relaxation

Could this be a disrespectful youngster sticking a tongue out at his teacher? No, actually, this is the action of licking and chewing, which indicates a horse is relaxed. A horse will not eat when frightened or aggressive, but when relaxed, a horse will often show his readiness to eat by moving his mouth and tongue. This yearling from Nevada in his first gentling session has relaxed ears, his head and neck are in a horizontal position (compare with Figure 1), and he is standing still facing his trainer—three displays of the body language of relaxation and respect.

Figure 4

Trust

The mustang mare and owner in Figure 4 have reached a high level of trust. Without restraints of any sort, she stands calmly and squarely facing her owner (a respectful distance away), there is a soft, gentle look in her eye, and her ears are up with interest. This body language shows a horse that is concentrating on her owner, and ready to learn.

Rewarding Your Mustang or Burro

Stroke your mustang gently and firmly as a reward during training, rather than giving treats by hand. Mustangs won't know what a treat is immediately and probably won't eat them at first. Hand feeding also encourages horses to nip. When you want to introduce your mustang to apples, carrots, and other healthy snacks, feed them to the horse in a bucket or trough. (Clicker training rewards may be an exception to this rule.) When your horse is gentled, keep hand-feeding of treats to a minimum, using positive verbal tones, scratches, and massaging as rewards instead.

Mustangs (and horses in general) don't enjoy being slapped or patted hard as a reward or greeting. If you observe horses interacting with one another, you will notice that horses show affection towards one another by using firm, methodical rubbing or grooming. Sudden, aggressive

Mother and daughter mustangs displaying mutual grooming, and the body language of affection.

actions will make them tense up and move away. Let your mustang sniff a new person's hand (maybe several times) before the person touches the horse, as you would with a dog. Don't let anyone slap or hit your mustang as a form of greeting or to show him "who is boss."

Adopting a Pair

If you adopt a mare, or a jenny with an unweaned foal at her side, you may find that she will be so preoccupied with keeping her baby safe from what she perceives as a predator (you) that she will run and encourage her foal to do the same whenever you approach. A mother should be given a safe home to nurture her baby without a lot of stress at first. (It is not uncommon, unfortunately, for a wild mare that is pregnant to abort her fetus while under the stress of gentling or training.)

Since a wild foal will often approach you out of curiosity more easi-

The author's mustang "Clay," progressing nicely in his halter training as a yearling with Bryan Neubert at the 1999 Horse and Burro show in Reno, Nevada.

ly, you may want to gentle the foal before its mother. (Feed the mare while you work with her foal, and stay alert for any sudden signs of aggression.) Foals have short attention spans and need to play, so make the lessons brief and fun. As your non-threatening behavior gains trust with the mare, she might relax her vigilance over her foal, and you can begin her gentling. If she cannot concentrate on you while her foal is near, wean the foal (at four to six months of age) before training the mare. The use of a "creep feeder" may be helpful in isolating the foal for training.

Training

After the gentling stage comes the training phase. Here the horse is taught to understand the meaning of the bridle, saddle, rider, (or harness, cart, and driver) and accompanying cues, aids and gaits. For your adopted mustang under the age of four, training tools and workouts are introduced but not strenuously applied. Only when a horse's leg joints

Desensitizing Cirrus, an older gelding to rope around girth area.

are mature (at age three or older) can they safely be worked hard or ridden. Your young horse may look mature enough, but have a vet or someone knowledgeable feel the joints to determine if they have fused.

A trainer needs to know the correct methods when schooling a horse. These can be found in books, videos, and from other experienced trainers, and are too lengthy to include here. Know what you are doing, and why, *before* training your horse, or you will start your horse out on the wrong foot, which will need correction later. If you hire a professional trainer, make sure they use non-forceful, horse psychology-based methods, and are willing to work with both you and your horse together. It is important that you are involved in your horse's training as much as possible to ensure consistency and good results when you are riding.

There are a lot of things you can do to desensitize your adopted mustang to the smell, feel, sight and sound of the equipment and actions needed for riding or driving. A desensitized animal will have much less trouble accepting a saddle and rider. Introduce the horse to every piece of new tack, mounting blocks, and handling that he or she requires before you or your trainer rides.

Standing Tied

The "standing tied" lesson is very important and can easily be done incorrectly. Before tying your animal to anything for the first time, take the lead-rope around a secure post or tree but continue to hold the end like a pulley. Hold tension when the horse pulls back to simulate the animal being tied, but if the animal panics, give it slack but do not allow it to get free. When it is calm again, take up the excess slack. When the horse or burro encounters resistance, your halter training of "giving to pressure" and being rewarded for forward movement will come in handy, and the animal should move forward to give itself slack in the rope. Give enough rope so that the horse can move its head around without feeling confined, but not enough so that it can put a foot over the rope and scare itself.

Use nylon yacht-test rope halters and yacht-rope leads that will not stretch or break and that contain no metal hardware. Keep working with your horse or burro until it no longer panics, sits back against the pressure, or tests the rope. Do not leave the animal standing tied by itself until this occurs. If the horse finds he or she can break the rope or halter, or can stretch the halter and turn its head and slip out, he or she may constantly test the rope when tied.

Teach your horse to stand tied to an immovable object such as a tree or a tall post set in concrete by wrapping an automobile or motorcycle inner-tube around the post, and tying the lead-rope to the tube. Always use a "quick release" type knot. Do not tie directly to a hard, unyielding object because if the horse panics and pulls back, damage to the neck and back will occur. Young horses will get bored and begin pawing sooner than older horses. Require them to stand tied for shorter periods of time, and reward them with release when they stand calmly.

Left: Trainer Allen Worth prepares Clay for his "first ride" by simulating the weight, feel and motion of a rider while still standing on the fence. Right: If the horse stands still and is calm, the trainer sits in the saddle while still holding onto the fence.

Use the Fence

Prepare your horse for the sound and motion of a rider by sitting on a fence your horse stands next to and laying the free end of the leadrope on its back, petting its neck, and patting the horse's back. Repeat on both sides of the horse until the horse is completely unafraid.

Simulate a Girth

A thick cotton rope moved back and forth in a see-saw motion, and eventually tightened up gently on a horse's girth or a surcingle will help the horse overcome the discomfort of something encircling its body. Repeat on both sides until the horse is completely unafraid.

Getting Used to Bridle, Blanket and Saddle

Desensitize your mustang to unfamiliar riding equipment by approaching the horse from the front, letting the horse see and sniff the object thoroughly (and perhaps mouth it a little), then rub it on his shoulder, and let him sniff it again. The saddle blanket, then the saddle, should be introduced in this way, and the horse gradually taught to accept their sound, motion, texture and smell, before laying them on the horse's back. Use a light saddle that you can easily remove. Do not tighten the girth until your horse is completely comfortable and stands still. Since many mustangs are smaller and have shorter backs than domestic horses, short, lightweight saddles such as Western cordura, Australian, barrel-racing, round skirt, English, or endurance saddles are good choices.

When the horse accepts the pad and saddle on its back, the saddle girth needs to be tightened up enough so the saddle won't slide underneath the horse's belly. *Expect a natural flight reaction* to girthing up for the first time (such as running, rearing, spooking, bucking, or kicking). Remove halter, lead or bridle and encourage the horse to run around freely inside a safe training pen for as long as it needs to become comfortable with the saddle on its back. Never immobilize a horse, or force it to accept bridle, pad, saddle or rider. A horse's trust in you will be broken if it is pushed further than its comfort level allows. When a horse is comfortable with a saddle, add inert weight and motion (such as a sack of grain or a large, soft floppy doll tied to the saddle) to accustom the horse to the motion and weight of a "rider," if you like.

A snaffle bridle is recommended for a horse in training, (with an "O," "D," or full-cheek snaffle bit). Allow the horse to smell and mouth the bridle before gently inserting the bit into the horse's mouth and over its tongue. (Warm the bit in your hand first!) There should be one wrinkle at the outside corner of the horse's mouth when placed properly. You may have to shorten or lengthen the bridle's cheekpieces to achieve this. Allow the horse to play with the bit until it learns it is most comfortable over the tongue, and in the open space between front and back teeth. Watch for "wolf teeth" which grow in the space needed for the bit, and have them removed by a veterinarian. A rawhide bosal (circular nosepiece) sidepull, or a halter can also be used for training if a bit is not desirable.

When a horse is mature physically, and completely desensitized to

From burro to police horse (left), mustangs and burros make calm, safe riding partners when trained correctly.

all equipment, motion, and sound, you can begin to accustom the horse to weight in the stirrups, and the feel of a rider stepping up into the stirrup, and then back down repeatedly (without actually putting a leg over). Unless you are experienced, however, do not do this without knowledgeable help. Riding a horse for the first time is potentially dangerous and requires knowing what to do, and why you are doing it in any given circumstance, and cannot be covered adequately here. Pushing a horse too fast, or applying the wrong methods at this stage may destroy the trust that took so long to build. Many sources of specific instruction and support in all the different types of riding are available, and should be used now. Congratulations—you and your mustang are well on your way to becoming successful riding partners. (Do not be surprised if after all this desensitization, your horse calmly accepts being saddled and ridden for the first time without batting an eye.) You may or may not want to take the first ride. If not, find an appropriate gentle trainer.

"Aerial," a BLM burro delights attendees at adoption in Roseville, California.

*"Lalo" the mustang
learns dressage!*

A wary, brown sabino-colored mustang yearling enters the gentling pen for the first time. Gentling demonstrations offered by professionals at adoptions can provide a definite benefit to wild horses and their new owners.

Riding in an Hour or Less

Don't do it! There are many videos or live demonstrations that show a wild horse being bridled, saddled and ridden in a short period of time— sometimes in an hour or less. In the hands of an expert, this is possible but should *never* be attempted by a novice. Every wild horse deserves to go through gentling, desensitization, and training gradually over a span of weeks, months, or longer. If you can have your horse gentled or "demo'd" at an adoption by a reputable trainer who has volunteered to help adopters, by all means take advantage of this. Your horse will be much easier to start at home. However, avoid allowing anyone to train your horse who wants to take shortcuts or use force or pain to ride a horse in a short period of time. The horse will tell you when it is calm enough to be ridden, and this varies with each horse and should be honored.

Trailer Training

After your horse can stand tied, introduce it slowly and calmly to the trailer. It is best to use a stock trailer with no dividers or feed bins, and have the trailer hooked up to the truck so it won't tip forward. Most stock trailers have a safety escape door on the side, which you should leave unlatched (but not wide open) in case you need to use it. You can lead a horse or burro into a trailer and use the safety door to exit, or you can teach your horse to move forward into the trailer by using a long line or very long lead-rope threaded through a window or upper slat and used to apply gentle pressure to the horse to step forward. As in training to lead, always give the horse slack in the rope if they panic, but do not allow them to escape. Have an assistant keep the horse heading straight into the open end of the trailer and away from the sides of the trailer. Reward *every* try that the horse makes, however slight, such as head down towards the trailer floor, sniffing the trailer, and finally stepping in completely with an immediate release of rope pressure. This can be a very long process and should never be given a time limit.

Practice trailering in and out calmly and take short practice runs before you need to trailer your horse for an actual ride. When the horse enters the trailer willingly and stands calmly, tie it with a regular-length lead-rope facing the middle of the road for best weight distribution. Make sure it has enough rope to move its head back and forth and up and down comfortably for balance. Always close the back door after tying a horse in a trailer. If a horse backs out and over the edge of the rear trailer door while still tied, it can hurt its legs severely. Always use a quick release knot and tie it so it can be easily reached from outside of the trailer. Make sure any excess lead-rope is "chained" on itself or shortened up so it does not catch on anything as you drive. Allowing a horse to turn around in a wide stock trailer and tying them facing backwards is fine, providing there is not a large space for it to stick its head out above the back door. Tie the horse so that it can't reach this space, or block the space with soft "snow-fence" or plywood.

Make trailering a positive experience. Give the horse treats for standing quietly tied in the trailer, limit the distance of trips at first, never allow injuries to occur, and your horse or burro will load and unload easily. Trailering is essential for long distance vet needs, off-site training,

"No Myth," a registered Spanish Mustang stallion, enjoys a good scratch from owner and buddy, Greg, from Wild Star Ranch in Texas. His color is bay sabino snowflake, with two blue eyes.

emergency evacuation, access to activities for fun and exercise, and should be a part of basic horse training.

Advanced or Specialized Training

After basic gentling and saddle training, when the horse is mature enough in body and mind, the horse's training can be expanded to include competitive trail riding, events, dressage, roping, or any equine skill you prefer. When your horse has a basic foundation and understanding in place, you can add more skills. You may decide to enter your horse in shows, or rely on him or her as a working partner. Avoid overwork and injuries. Your partnership can be healthy and positive for a lifetime if you are sensitive to your horse's needs. You can also function as a wild horse or burro "ambassador" to show the world what these animals can achieve! The BLM may want well-trained horses and their owners to appear at expositions, fairs, and to help promote adoptions. Answering questions and showing off your hard work to the public can be very rewarding, especially when it educates more people about the abilities of these animals.

Obtaining Certificate of Title

For the first year, your adopted mustang remains the property of the BLM. At the end of the year, when you must pass an inspection to determine if you have cared for the horse properly, you will be issued a certificate of ownership. You cannot sell or give away a mustang before you have a certificate of ownership.

Even when titled, mustangs (or any horse) should never be sold for slaughter. Every attempt should be made to place a horse in a caring home if you absolutely cannot keep it. The BLM has re-adopt programs where they will take back your untitled horse and find another adopter. The internet, local newspapers or horse magazines all have classified ads where people are looking to buy horses. Mustang clubs, or your local riding or 4-H club may help you find another home for your horse. Take color photos and make an attractive poster with a list of the horse's good qualities to place in local feed and tack stores, grocery stores, and other public bulletin boards. Some organizations such as boy's and girl's ranches, summer camps, or therapeutic riding programs take donations of trained horses, or horse non-profit rescue groups and sanctuaries may be able to help you.

You can retain ownership of your titled mustang if you lease it out to another person in a "maintenance" arrangement. The lessee pays nothing for the animal, but does pay for feed and maintenance expenses like hoof care, worming, dental work and vaccinations. You should write up a legal contract with all possible considerations included such as who pays for vet care, who transports the horse back to you, the time span, and what stipulates a breach of contract. Specify that the horse must be kept in a location accessible to you. Visit the horse and keep in contact with the lessee. Often this arrangement is good for leasing a small horse to a child who will outgrow it. Smaller mustangs are a good size for children, but they must be completely gentled and trained to be safe.

Prepare to make a lifetime commitment to an adopted animal. If you

Off into the sunset, wild horses in Nevada.
Opposite page: Mustangs can become closely bonded to those they trust.

must find it a new home, make sure you find someone who is knowledgeable, kind, and able to afford to care for it. If your mustang or burro becomes terminally ill or injured beyond rehabilitation it is your responsibility to allow it to die in comfort and peace, or have a vet humanely euthanize it. Never reward a horse or burro's companionship by sending it suffering or old to an auction or slaughterhouse. There are many equine rescue organizations that may take horses in need, which will give you peace of mind should you be unable to keep your animal.

Your Very
Own Mustang

Mustang Trivia

A "Medicine Hat" pinto. Some Native American tribes believed horses with colored areas over the ears and eyes (war bonnets), and chest, flanks, and base of tail (war shields) like this mustang in New Mexico, were magically protected from battle injuries, as was the person who rode them.

🐎 The only survivor (on the losing side) found on the battlefield after "Custer's Last Stand" was a 14-year-old half-mustang cavalry horse named Comanche, ridden by a Captain Miles Keogh. Comanche was discovered alive and bleeding from six wounds, but recovered, and was kept as a 7th Cavalry mascot. With strict orders not to be ridden or struck, he was regularly fed whiskey bran mashes and buckets of beer. He lived to be 29.

🐎 Trained mustangs are present everywhere domestic horses are ridden or shown. You've probably seen them but didn't know they were once wild, unless you noticed the freezebrands. (Ask at a National BLM Office for free trading cards of "famous" mustangs and burros shown in dressage, endurance, reining, jumping, driving, and military events.)

🐎 Some mustangs mature later in life or are smaller than domestic horses because of the poor nutrition they started out with on the range. Mustangs have been known to continue growing in height until five or six years old when provided with high-quality food.

Short, bony and bigheaded, Indian pony mustangs (this one ridden by young Cree Indians) could nevertheless outrun and outlast taller, more muscular horses.

In the 1800s, Plains Indians mounted on sure-footed mustangs under 14 hands easily outran and outlasted the larger, heavier, grain-fed horses of the U.S. Cavalry, and were reported to "go ninety miles without food or water."

The calm, gentle donkey's name comes from the Middle English combination of *dun* (the color) and *key* (small animal). The word "burro" is a variation (referring to a smaller donkey) of the Spanish word "borrico."

Since many mustangs possess fine problem-solving skills from surviving on the range, it is advisable to keep your mustang's gates closed with a chain and a horse-resistant snap.

Two variations of the most frequent horse color, bay: red bay, left; and blood bay, right; as seen at the Palomino Valley Holding Facility.

Donkeys are drought-resistant and, like the camel, only drink as much water as their body tissues need and no more. Their earliest origins were in the deserts of Egypt, Nubia, Ethiopia, and the Somali Coast of Africa. Donkeys have no body odor, even when sweating.

Burros were brought to the Americas by the Spanish. They were used not only to transport cargo, but were essential in the breeding of mules (the sterile offspring of a horse and a burro). Today's wild burros are descendents of animals that escaped or were turned loose by early miners and sheepherders. The deserts of California, Arizona, and Nevada suit their survival needs perfectly.

Mustangs are far less affected by osteochondrosis, a disease found within one or several developing joints in some young horses, which is a serious problem for domestic horse breeds. In general, mustangs have been found to have healthier hooves, teeth, bones, and possess greater stamina than domestic horses.

The word "pinto" describes a pattern of color and white existing on any breed of horse, including mustangs. In describing a pinto mustang, it is helpful to know the difference between the two most common pinto patterns—"tobiano" and "overo." (See below.) Tobianos have more regularly-shaped patches, and the white areas on the horse start on the back and spread downward as if white paint were poured downward on top of the horse. The head is usually dark, but the legs are usually white. An overo, on the other hand, shows smaller patches of white that are more ragged and irregular. The face is almost always white, and the legs mostly dark. An overhead view of an overo should show more dark color along the topline. Some mustangs have a color variation called "sabino," which is comprised of two or more high white stockings (over the knee or hock), a bald face, and white on the belly and sometimes on the sides.

TWO MOST COMMON TYPES OF PINTOS:

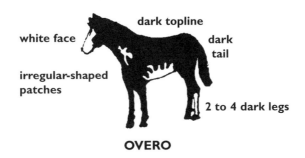

OVERO

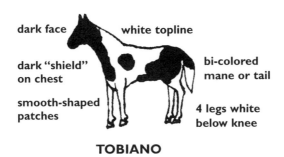

TOBIANO

🐎 Only seven species of the genus *Equus* remain out of the 250 that have evolved over millions of years. Those remaining are *Equus caballus* (the domestic horse), *Equus praewalski* (Przewalski's Horse), *Equus asinus* (African ass—burro or donkey), *Equus hemiouus* (Asian ass—onager), *Equus zebra* (Mountain zebra), *Equus burchelli* (Common zebra), and *Equus grevyi* (Grevy's zebra). All species except the domestic horse and common zebra are listed as endangered.

🐎 Spanish horses brought to the New World were suspended on the decks of the galleons in big, canvas slings that supported their bellies, tethered by their front feet to the deck, halter leadropes tied to a rail, and the horse's rear end positioned directly above the ocean for easy "stall" cleaning! Only half the Spanish horses lived through these voyages, however. These select survivors became the predecessors of today's tough, enduring mustangs.

🐎 In the 1800s, herds of wild mustangs were captured by Indians over a period of several weeks in the following way. A small group of prospective horse owners would desensitize the herd to their presence by speaking softly to them, then gradually add more stimulus every day until they could make a great deal of noise and wave blankets without the horses paying any attention. The Indians then constructed a long corral at the end of a nearby box canyon, and the herd was first calmly maneuvered, and then abruptly stampeded into the trap.

🐎 The BLM freezebrand found on the left side of every mustang's neck is a code (read left to right) for "US," the year of the horse's birth, and the horse's registration number. Liquid nitrogen lowers the temperature of the branding iron to 300 degrees below zero, which is less painful than using a "red hot" branding iron.

🐎 Blue eyes are commonly found in pintos or other mustangs with white pigment near or over the eye. There is no problem with vision simply because a horse has a blue (sometimes called a "glass") eye. However, any horse with white patches (and pink skin underneath them) will be more subject to sunburn and skin cancer. (If you own one of these horses, apply sunscreen in the summer!)

🐎 Horses are not totally colorblind. The colors they seem to see best are green and yellow.

🐎 Wild stallions are sometimes observed preferring to breed with mares of a similar color on the range. You might think this would produce herds of the same color, eventually, but most colors do not "breed true." Studies of horse color genetics show many "surprise" colors appear in foals. Here are some genetic rules that have been tested and proven:

- Breeding two black horses usually makes black foals, but occasionally you get a chestnut or a bay.

- Bay horses breed true about half the time, the other half will be chestnut or black.

- Brown and brown will give you chestnuts as well as browns.

- When two greys breed (greys are born dark brown or black, and then turn grey, then white as they age), there's a 75 percent chance you will get a grey foal.

- Roan horses (white hairs mixed with bay equals "red roan," with chestnut equals "strawberry roan," and with black equals "blue roan") three-fourths of the time produce roan foals.

- Palomino and palomino will make either palomino, cream-colored or chestnut foals (or an occasional red dun.)

- Red dun plus red dun will give you red dun or chestnut.

- Buckskins bred together will always produce buckskins, bays, *and* cream-colored offspring.

- In order to produce a pinto foal, one of the parents must be a pinto. Overo genes produce overos, and tobiano genes produce tobianos.

- Cream and cream will give you nothing but cream-colored foals.

- Chestnut plus chestnut always equals chestnut.

Above: BLM burros for adoption in Roseville, California.

Below: Calm and curious, these burros await adoption at Palomino Valley, Nevada. Shown are spotted, black, and grey burros.

Where the Wild Ones Roam:

A State-by-State Guide

Arizona

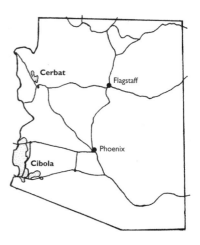

Highway 160, running across the top of the state east to west (also becoming Highways 98, 89 and 389) yields a bounty of horse sightings as it meanders delightfully through Navajo lands. You will see pintos, palominos, buckskins and more against sun-baked red mesas under brilliant blue skies.

Running free in herds on private Native American Indian land, these horses have become semi-wild, but they are not BLM mustangs. This is an inspirational area for photos or painting. (Gas stations and convenience stores are rare, so watch the tank and your H_2O!)

Large numbers of wild BLM horses are scarce here, but Arizona is wild *burro* country! Watch for these endearing, bunny-eared creatures everywhere. Domesticated wild burros make great pets, riding and packing animals. Gentling is as easy (if not easier) than with their cousin, the horse. Burros have been known to pick up dogs with their teeth and throw them, so don't mix these two species right away! Burros will also guard pastures against coyotes.

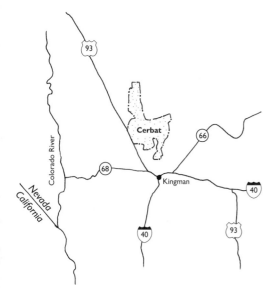

Northwestern

Cerbat HMA is 5 miles north of Kingman, AZ, on US 93 east of the road. The historic mining town of Chloride sits at the western base of this HMA. About 70 horses are all that are left here. This small, isolated herd is known for its original Spanish Colonial blood. These horses are high in the mountains and are rarely (if ever) seen. The BLM has protected their status and given them isolation to breed. They are mostly roan, bay or chestnut-colored.

The town of **Oatman, AZ**, is on Route 66. Ten to 12 wild burros visit Oatman at the same time every day. Do not give the burros junk food — just pellets and carrots, please!

Southwestern

Cibola-Trigo HMA lies in the Sonoran Desert, between the towns of Yuma and Quartzite, and again on Interstate Highway 8 between Yuma and Gila Bend. Wild horses are most likely to be seen along Highway 95 between the southern boundary of the Yuma Proving Ground (YPG) military base and Martinez Lake Road at approximately mile post 56 (about 10 miles north of YPG). Along the northern portion of the HMA, horses are found along the Colorado River off US 95, and west on Cibola Lake Road for approximately 45 miles. A large portion of this HMA lies within the YPG, which is closed to the public. Horses and burros cross Highway 95 at night, especially in the winter, so be careful. There are approximately 125 horses here—mostly bays, blacks, and also some appaloosas—and about six times as many burros!

South Central

Native American horse herds have been spotted on the **Gila Indian Reservation** south of Phoenix, along Highway 347 between Riggs Road and Highway 238, and along Riggs Road (a.k.a. Beltline Road) between Interstate 10 and the Sierra Estrella Mountains. The best times for sightings are dawn and dusk.

For more Arizona Wild Horse and Burro information contact:
BLM Arizona State Office
222 N. Central Ave.
Phoenix, AZ 85004-2203
(602) 417-9200
www.az.blm.gov

BLM Kingman Resource Area Office(Cerbat HMA)
2475 Beverly Ave.
Kingman, AZ 86401
(520) 692-4400
www.az.blm.gov/whb/cerbathma.htm

BLM Yuma Field Office (Cibola-Trigo HMA)
2555 E. Gila Ridge Road
Yuma, AZ 85365-2240
(520) 317-3200
www.az.blm.gov/whb/cibolahma.htm

Oatman, AZ burros:
www.route66azlastingimpressions.com/Oatman_Burros

To volunteer:
Contact BLM Phoenix District Office: (602) 580-5500

"Clippy," a purple roan mustang (and registered American Indian Horse) with a sense of humor, enjoys removing Joel's hat—and throwing it.

Wild horses graze in front of visitors at the overnight camp at Shingletown, California.

Litchfield Corrals offers many fine mustangs for adoption, including this uniquely colored pair: a snowflake black mare and her red bay "splashed white" pinto foal.

"Walk-n-Trot's California Girl," a well-groomed, well-trained palomino mustang is shown at the 1999 Horse Expo in Sacramento, California.

California

Horses were brought to California when Spain colonized lands in the 1700s. During the early 1830s, California reportedly was "swarming" with herds of wild horses. During the late 1840s Gold Rush, bands of mustangs on the western side of the San Joaquin Valley were said to contain anywhere from 200 to 2000 horses!

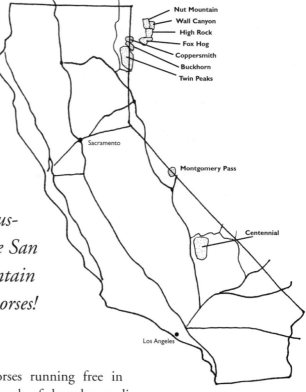

The demise of wild horses running free in California came at the hands of drought conditions, and man. Sadly, huge numbers of wild horses were driven over ocean cliffs to their deaths to stop them from grazing on land wanted for livestock. Today, free-roaming mustangs are found in high, forested mountains, the arid desert, and in a few large sanctuaries. California has two BLM holding facilities for horses and burros, and the BLM holds adoptions in many California cities.

Northern

Sixteen miles east of Susanville, CA, on Highway 395, the public may view mustangs at the **BLM Litchfield Corrals Adoption and Holding Facility**. View the horses, make an appointment to adopt, or attend an auction of horses gentled by inmates at the nearby California Correctional Center. The Correctional Center gentles and trains the horses for 90 days, and an adoption is held every three months for about 20 horses.

More than 600 wild horses, burros and a few wild mules were counted in 1997 in the **Twin Peaks HMA**, 25 miles northeast of Susanville, CA. Bordering this approximately 798,000-acre HMA to the west is Highway 395; to the north are the Warner Mountains; to the south is Honey Lake

Valley; and to the east, the border lies in the Smoke Creek Desert of Nevada. Smoke Creek bisects the HMA and is the main water source. Horses have been observed from vehicles driven on Smoke Creek Road near a spring about a quarter of a mile south of the road, and on a steep hillside approximately one mile west of Bull Flat. Rush Mountain, Shinn Mountain, Skedaddle Mountain, and the Three Springs area are locations where many horses are seen, including appaloosas, grays, blacks, pintos and buckskins.

Above Twin Peaks HMA are the smaller **Coppersmith** and **Buckhorn HMAs**. Coppersmith lies approximately 10 miles south of Eagleville, CA, with Buckhorn directly below. Nearly 100 horses roam each of the smaller HMAs, with cavalry remount characteristics such as quarter horse and Morgan blood. Bay, black and brown colors predominate.

Five miles north of Alturas, CA, the **Devil's Garden Wild Horse Territory** lies within Modoc National Forest. A tiny border of the territory parallels Highway 395 at the Highway 299 (Cedarville) exit. These 236,000 acres contain about 250 horses with draft characteristics such as large size and feathering on their legs.

The **Wild Horse Sanctuary** near Shingletown, CA, is a private 5,000-acre sanctuary where wild horses and burros may be viewed by the public as they live out their lives in peace. Approximately 300 horses separated into many small family groups can be seen during an unforgettable horseback ride and overnight stay at the comfortable campsite (complete with grilled meals). The Sanctuary is located between Highways 36 and 44, about 25 miles east of Red Bluff and Redding. Reservations are needed for trail rides.

California

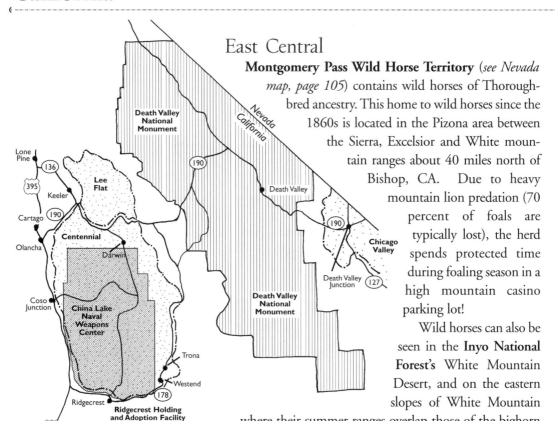

East Central

Montgomery Pass Wild Horse Territory (*see Nevada map, page 105*) contains wild horses of Thoroughbred ancestry. This home to wild horses since the 1860s is located in the Pizona area between the Sierra, Excelsior and White mountain ranges about 40 miles north of Bishop, CA. Due to heavy mountain lion predation (70 percent of foals are typically lost), the herd spends protected time during foaling season in a high mountain casino parking lot!

Wild horses can also be seen in the **Inyo National Forest's** White Mountain Desert, and on the eastern slopes of White Mountain where their summer ranges overlap those of the bighorn sheep on the crest of the mountain. **Rock Creek Pack Station**, in conjunction with the University of California at Davis, operates mustang observation pack trips on horseback through this area in summer. Learn about mustangs, soak in the hot tub, and camp under the stars in Inyo National Forest.

Highway 190 contains a tiny town named **Death Valley Junction** (the last chance to head north before the "inferno" of Death Valley!). On the highway running through town, you will see the "Drive Slowly—Wild Horse Crossing" sign, and the small herd that regularly strolls in front of stopped cars and trucks on their way to feed and water at the home of a local resident. They can be approached and photographed, but please don't try to touch!

Southeastern

Nearly 300 horses live inside the **Centennial HMA**. Comprised of nearly one million acres between Death Valley National Monument to the east and Highway 395 to the west, a large portion of the HMA is in the inaccessible China Lake Naval Weapons Center. However, the northern border along Highway 190 contains public land for horse watching. Places to see horses are along Highway 178 between the town of Westend to the south and the intersection with Highway 190 to the north.

BLM **Ridgecrest Holding and Adoption Facility** is 4.5 miles east of Ridgecrest, CA, on Highway 178. Adoptions are by appointment only, but you can visit anytime. The hours are M-F, 7-4. If you visit when the office is closed, you can still circle the perimeter and see the horses. Up to 1,500 horses and burros can be held on the facility's 50 acres. Ridgecrest usually has all colors and sizes of wild burros for adoption, including spotted, gray, black, and pink burros!

For more California Wild Horse and Burro information contact:
BLM California Law Enforcement Hotline (to report CA wild horse or burro abuse): 1-800-545-4256

BLM California State Office
2800 Cottage Way, Suite W1834
Sacramento, CA 95825-0451
(916) 978-4400
www.ca.blm.gov
www.wildhorseandburro.blm.gov/adpsch.html

BLM Eagle Lake Field Office (Twin Peaks HMA)
2950 Riverside Drive
Susanville, CA 96130
(530) 257-0456

BLM Litchfield Adoption and Holding Facility
Highway 395
Susanville, CA
(800) 545-4256

BLM Ridgecrest Field Office (Centennial HMA)
300 S. Richmond Road
Ridgecrest, CA 93555
(760) 384-5400

BLM Ridgecrest Adoption and Holding Facility
Highway 178
Ridgecrest, CA
800-951-8720
www.equinenet.org/life/whbridgecrest.html

BLM Surprise Field Office (Buckhorn, Coppersmith, Fox Hog, and High Rock HMAs)
602 Cressler Street
Cedarville, CA 96104
(530) 279-6101

BLM Susanville Office (CA Correctional Facility Inmate/Wild Horse Program)
2950 Riverside Dr.
Susanville, CA 96130
(530) 257-0456

Rock Creek Pack Station—Inyo National Forest mustang trips: winter phone: (760) 872-8331; summer phone: (760) 935-4493

University of California at Davis Summer Mustang Trips, "Mustangs: A Living Legacy":
(800) 752-0881 or (530) 757-8899

The Wild Horse Sanctuary (Shingletown, CA):
(530) 335-2241; www.wildhorsesanctuary.org

To volunteer:
BLM Bakersfield District Office: (661) 391-6049; email: modom@ca.blm.gov
BLM Eagle Lake Resource Office: (916) 257-5381; email: lhansen@ca.blm.gov
BLM Ridgecrest Resource Office: (760) 384-5430; email: dsjaasta@ca.blm.gov
BLM State Office: (916) 978-4400; email: rfagan@ca.blm.gov

Colorado

Southern

Wild horses at the **BLM Canon City Holding Facility** are available for adoption twice a month for qualified adopters with appointments. They can be halter-trained and gelded for an additional cost by the BLM in conjunction with the **Colorado Department of Corrections' Wild Horse Inmate Program** (WHIP) at the prison. Minimum-security prisoners (see *Mother Jones* magazine,

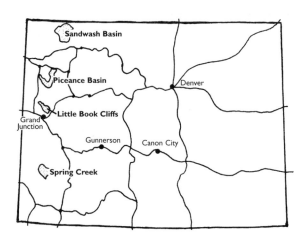

March/April 2001) are matched with just three mustangs at a time and use "resistance-free" training methods. Saddle-trained mustangs can also be adopted from the WHIP and BLM for $855 per gelding, and $780 per mare, plus the adoption fee of $125. Adopters and trained horses are matched in regards to skill level and suitability. Burros are also available for adoption. The training is quiet and careful, with true appreciation for each horse.

Southwest

Fifty or so wild horses, their ancestors bred as cavalry mounts, still run through the **Spring Creek HMA** in the Disappointment Valley south of Naturita, CO (at Highway 90 west of Montrose). The best place to see horses is near water sources such as springs, creeks and water tanks. From Durango, take US 160 to 666 west past Dove Creek to the Colorado 141 turnoff. Travel north on 141 through Egnar and Slick Rock. Just before Gypsum Gap, turn south off 141 onto County Road 19Q, and go 5.2 miles. Turn east on BLM road 4010 and go about 3.5 miles to the HMA entrance. (Rattlesnakes are common here, so be careful where you step!)

West Central

Little Bookcliffs Wild Horse Range is a mustang refuge near Grand Junction, CO. In the past, the BLM has added more pinto, palomino, buckskin, and roan mustang stallions to produce more colorful horses. Many different trails and difficulty levels wind through this park, but the most accessible and easy are Coal Canyon and Main Canyon. The gate is open June through November (but closed from December 1 to May 31 to protect wintering and foaling areas). The Coal Canyon entrance to Little Bookcliffs is found on Highway 70 near the Palisade exit (about 20 miles east of Grand Junction). The Coal Canyon entrance is the best place to go for easiest hikes or rides into the park, and the best place to view horses in the wintertime. Other locations for good mustang watching are the Indian Park entrance, and in the North Soda area. Horseback riders, hikers, bikers, and motor vehicle sightseers share the wide dirt roads with the bands of wild horses.

Northwest

BLM Mustang herds are also found in two other, more isolated herd management areas of Colorado. The **Piceance Basin HMA** (pronounced Pee-ants) contains around 100 mustangs accessible by rough dirt roads shared with oil and gas exploration, and cattle grazing. Go 19 miles north on Highway 13 from Rifle, CO. Turn west on Piceance Creek Road (CR-5) to Ryan Gulch Road (#24). In the spring, the best place to view horses is at 84 Mesa and along Yellow Creek. In the summer, the horses move to higher elevations. In general, look for horses along the face of Cathedral Bluffs. Watch for bad road conditions and beware of flash flooding in creek beds during summer thunderstorms.

Colorado

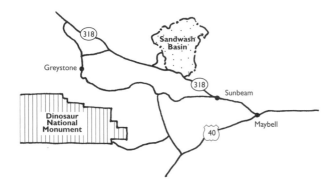

The **Sandwash Basin HMA** (the largest HMA in Colorado with 160,000 acres) lies between Vermillion Bluffs and Sevenmile Ridge, with Monument Hill a landmark when entering from the south. This is an interesting geological area with Dinosaur National Monument nearby to the west. The 200 or so colorful mustangs roaming this semi-arid canyonland tend to be tall and heavy. Go 31 miles west of Craig to Maybell. Continue northwest from Maybell on Highway 318 for 17 miles to the southern entrance. (Tours of this area may be available through a local organization called Maverick Mustangs.)

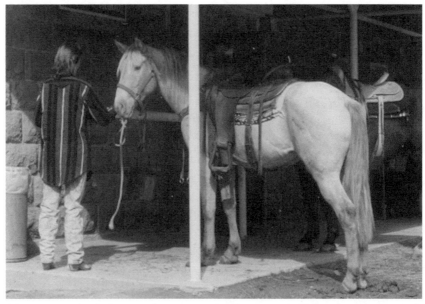

Training completed, this rare champagne-colored mustang (with hazel eyes) is reunited with his admiring owner at Canon City, Colorado's Prison Wild Horse and Inmate Program.

For more Colorado Wild Horse and Burro Information

BLM Colorado State Office
2850 Youngfield Street
Lakewood, CO 80215
(303) 239-3600
www.co.blm.gov/wildhb

BLM Canon City Field Holding and Adoption Facility/
    W.H.I.P. Program
3170 East Main
Canon City, CO 81215
(719) 269-8500
www.co.blm.gov/wildhb/ccwhtrain.htm

BLM Little Snake Field Office (Sandwash Basin HMA)
455 Emerson Street
Craig, CO 81625
(970) 826-5000

BLM San Juan Field Office (Spring Creek HMA)
15 Burnett Court
Durango, CO 81301
(970) 274-4874
www.co.blm.gov/sjra-horse3.htm

BLM White River Field Office (Piceance HMA)
73544 Highway 64
Meeker, CO 81641
(970) 878-3601

BLM Grand Junction Field Office (Little Bookcliffs Wild Horse
    Range)
2815 H Road
Grand Junction, CO 81506
(970) 244-3000
www.co.blm.gov/gjra/lbc.htm

Maverick Mustangs (Sandwash Basin HMA Wild Horse Tours):
    (970) 824-3868; www.maverick-mustang.com/

To volunteer:
BLM Canon City Office: (719) 269-8500; email:
    fackley@co.blm.gov

"Sir Lancelot," a drafthorse-type dappled palomino mustang, from Colorado's Sandwash Basin HMA, is proudly displayed by his owner.

Georgia

Cumberland Island, managed by the National Park Service, is home to approximately 250 wild horses. Ancestors of horses from early settlers said to have been on the island since 1742 share the space with offspring of other mustangs, appaloosas, retired circus horses and Tennessee Walkers added since 1940.

Located south of Brunswick, GA, and east of Interstate 95, this National Seashore can be reached by ferry from the town of St. Mary's, GA (off Interstate 95 onto State Highway 40, right above the Florida/Georgia state line). Stay for the day or overnight in campsites on this 18-mile-long National Seashore island.

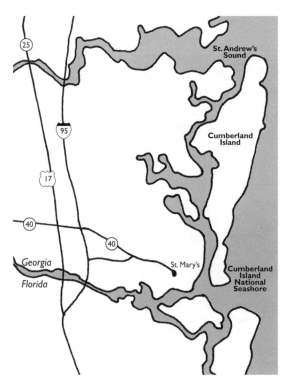

For more Georgia Wild Horse and Burro information contact:
BLM Southeastern States Office
Jackson Field Office
411 Briarwood Drive, Suite 404
Jackson, MS 39206
(601) 977-5400

Wild Horse & Burro Toll-Free: 1-866-4mustangs

Cumberland Island National Seashore: (912) 882-4336

Hawaii

On the Big Island of Hawaii, you can find wild horses inhabiting the lush Waipi'o Valley on the northeast coast.

Big Island

Isolated and contained by the ocean and high cliff walls, wild horses said to have been first let loose by early Spanish settlers can be seen if you are lucky. **Na'alapa Stables** will take you on a horseback tour of this lovely valley, complete with many stream crossings on capable trail horses of Spanish ancestry to try and find the elusive wild ones. Even if you don't find them, the valley more than suffices in beauty. Visitors and local residents report awakening on nearby beaches after overnight camping to see wild horses lying nearby! Some valley residents regularly feed the small bands that roam amid the coffee and taro farms.

West Central Big Island

On the other side of the Big Island, on Highway 19 eight miles north of Keahoe Airport, a "**Donkey Crossing**" sign warns drivers to watch for wild donkeys at "dawn and twilight hours." Originally brought by Spanish settlers, the wild burros of this area graze and water near the irrigated coast, then travel back across the highway to higher ground.

Na'alapa Stables at Waipi'o trail ride:
(808) 775-0419

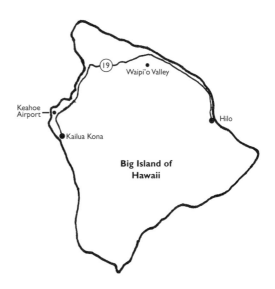

Where the
Wild Ones Roam

Idaho

Gray Percheron draft horse stallions were turned loose to mix with the mustangs in central Idaho, resulting in the larger build and gray coloration still seen today.

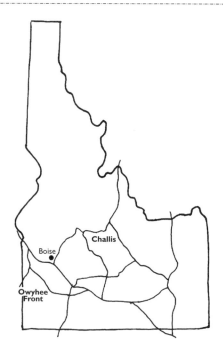

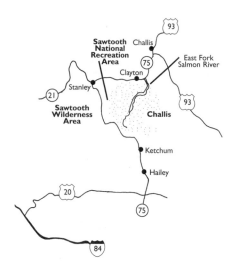

Central

Challis HMA, roughly 150 miles northeast of Boise on State Highway 75, has the largest number of wild horses in Idaho. The horse herds are on the east fork of the Salmon River. The larger size and grey coloration of these horses show their Grey Percheron stallion ancestry. In 1976, a BLM gather was opposed, and actor Lorne Greene (of *Bonanza* TV show fame) spoke publicly against the gather. There were more than 500 wild horses in Challis in 1976 when the roundup was stopped. The herd then increased to 660, but in 1978, the BLM won a court battle and the right to remove horses. The Challis herd numbers about 250 today.

Southwestern

The **Owyhee Front HMA** encompasses about 120,000 acres and contains about 150 horses. Traveling south on Interstate 84, exit onto US 95 south and go past Homedale to Marsing. Turn onto US 78 at Marsing, and travel through the Snake River Valley to reach this HMA. Near the Reynolds River, a paved road crosses the Owyhee Front HMA going south. The BLM recommends that you "keep the wind to your face and sun to your back" so

the horses will not smell you or see you as easily. They also warn against bringing noxious weed seeds into the area—unwittingly carried on one's clothing or in vehicles that might displace the native grasses the horses depend on.

For more Idaho Wild Horse and Burro information contact:
BLM Idaho State Office
1387 S. Vinnell Way
Boise, ID 83709-1657
(208) 373-4000
www.id.blm.gov/

BLM Owyhee Field Office
3948 Development Ave.
Boise, ID 83705
(208) 384-3300

BLM Challis Field Office
HC 63, Box 1670
Challis, ID 83226
(208) 879-4181

To volunteer:
BLM Owyhee Field Office:
    (208) 384-3300

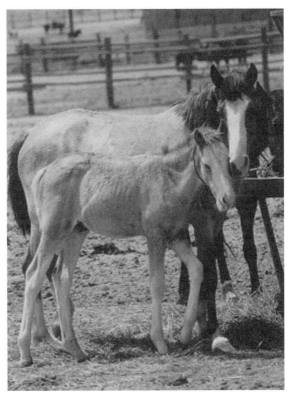

American mustangs come in rare colors such as this lilac roan mare and her chestnut sabino colt awaiting adoption at a holding facility.

Maryland and Virginia

Two herds of "Chincoteague Horses" inhabit Assateague Island, which is separated into Maryland (northern) and Virginia (southern) portions by a fence. These horses reportedly descend from Spanish stock

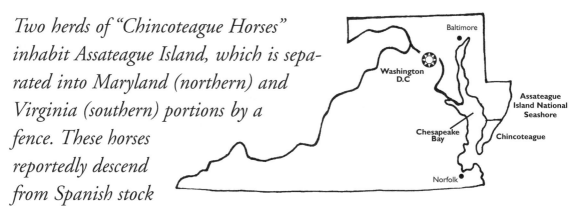

that swam ashore from a shipwrecked Spanish galleon.

Robust and healthy, these small, often colorful horses roam free and frolick in the tide. Their short stature is thought to be partly from their ancestry, and partly from their island diet. There is an annual auction at low tide held in July. The horses are driven swimming through the channel to be sold on smaller, nearby Chincoteague Island. This is a popular summer event, and all horses are usually adopted.

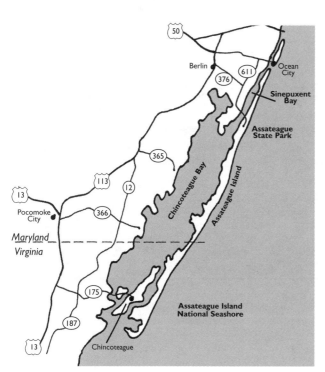

Assateague State Park and **Assateague Island National Seashore Recreational Area** can be reached by taking Highway 376 to 611 east of Berlin, MD, across Sinepuxent Bay. **Chincoteague Island** is accessible from Highway 175 off Highway 13.

For more Maryland & Virginia Wild Horse and Burro information contact:
BLM Southeastern States Jackson Field Office
411 Briarwood Drive, Suite 404
Jackson, MS 39206
(601) 977-540; (800) 293-1781

BLM Eastern States Office
7450 Boston Boulevard
Springfield, VA 22153
(703) 440-1700

Assateague Island National Seashore:
(410) 641-3030

Montana

Isolated from intro-duced stock, these horses have unique colorations — yellow-ish or mouse-grey with black stripes on their legs, down their backs, and across their shoulders, black manes, tails, legs, and black hooves.

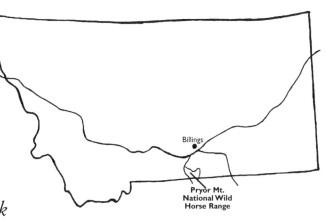

Located about 60 miles south of Billings, MT, The **Pryor Mountain Wild Horse Range** lies between Bighorn Canyon National Recreation Area to the northeast, Custer National Forest to the north-west, and BLM public lands to the west. The second public wild horse range to be established in the U.S. (1968), this 23,000-acre wild horse area includes fencing to keep horses in and other graz-ers out. Because this site was isolated from intro-duced stock, horses with the "dun factor" similar to the Kigers in Oregon and the Sulphurs in Utah have been allowed to continue to breed unchanged from earlier Spanish and American Indian horses since the 1890s. Pryor Mountain mustangs are prized as primitive, Spanish-type mustangs whose rarity must be protected and maintained, along with other unusual colors here such as nonline-backed duns, and sabinos.

Many of these colorful horses can be viewed along Bad Pass Highway (Highway 37) within the **Bighorn Canyon National Recreation Area.** Look for horses in the low-elevation lands north of the Mustang Flat interpretive sign. An area sur-rounding Penn's cabin (at the top of East Pryor

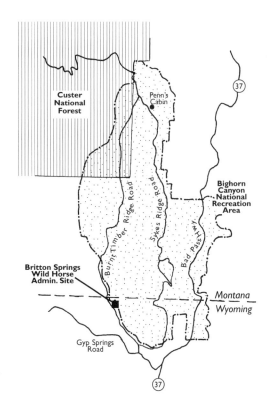

Montana

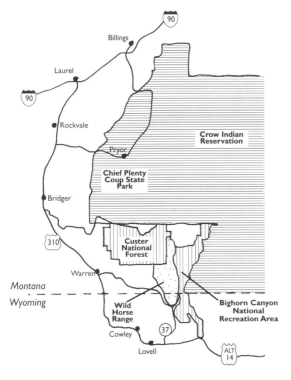

Mountain) can be accessed by off-road vehicle on Sykes Ridge Road or Burnt Timber Range Road, and yields the most mustang herd sightings. These horses have been extensively studied and photographed because of their color and herd dynamics.

For more Montana Wild Horse and Burro information contact:
BLM Montana, N Dakota, S Dakota Field Office
PO Box 36800
5001 Southgate Drive
Billings, MT 59107-6800
(406) 896-5004
www.mt.blm.gov

Pryor Mt. Wild Horse Refuge webpage:
www.webcom.com/~ladyhawk/breeding.html

To volunteer:
BLM Billings Field Office: (406) 896-5013; email:
lcmarkle@mt.blm.gov

Grulla color (also seen on these Kiger fillies in Oregon) is found on Pryor Mt. horses. This coloration always includes a dorsal stripe, darker head, legs, mane and tail than the body shade, and often leg stripes.

Although Nebraska has no wild horse herds roaming its lands, you can view and adopt western wild horses and burros at a BLM facility north of Elm Creek.

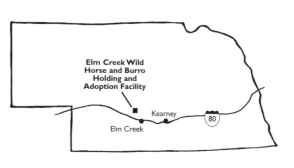

The BLM brings wild horses to the midwest via **Elm Creek Holding and Adoption Facility** located seven miles north of Interstate 80 on Highway 183 (exit 257). (When you go through the town of Elm Creek, you are halfway there.) The facility is open Monday through Friday, 8 AM to 4:30 PM and holds about 600 mustangs and burros captured in western states en route to adoptions in the midwest and eastern states.

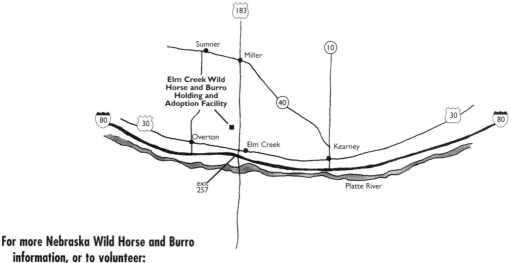

For more Nebraska Wild Horse and Burro information, or to volunteer:
BLM Nebraska and Wyoming State Office
5353 Yellowstone Road
PO Box 1828
Cheyenne, WY 82003
(307) 775-6256
www.wy.blm.gov

BLM Elm Creek Wild Horse Adoption and Holding
Facility: (308) 856-4498

Nevada

In 1910, there were nearly 100,000 free-roaming wild horses in Nevada—more horses than citizens! Today there are still about 24,000 mustangs on federal, state, and private lands, making Nevada truly the mustang-watcher's "jackpot" state!

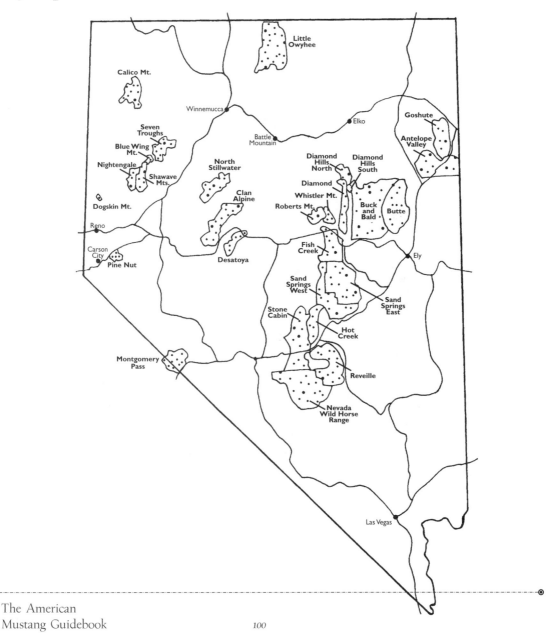

Lovely mares await adoption at the Palomino Valley Adoption and Holding Facility. The colors shown here are (left to right) golden wild bay, blue roan, black, chestnut, and chestnut tobiano pinto.
Right: Wild stallions for adoption at Palomino Valley Holding Facility

North Central

The 460,128-acre scenic **Little Owyhee Desert HMA**, the center of which is located 40 miles northeast of Winnemucca, NV, is too large to visit in one day. A haven for wild horses, this HMA is located in a remote part of the state. The north end of the HMA can be reached from the town of McDermitt on the Nevada-Oregon border via a scenic dirt road along the East Fork of the Quinn River. This road is not generally passable until late spring or summer. Camping is allowed anywhere on the HMA, with a

recommended primitive site at Twin Valley Springs. There are over 500 horses presently in the HMA, with numerous pintos in the southern portion.

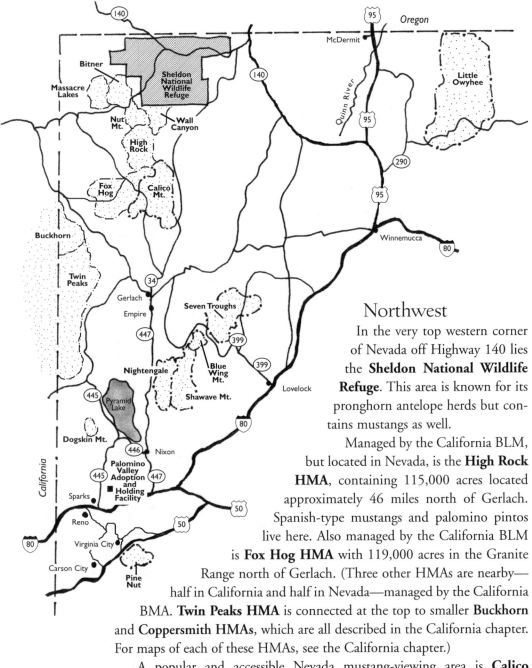

Northwest

In the very top western corner of Nevada off Highway 140 lies the **Sheldon National Wildlife Refuge**. This area is known for its pronghorn antelope herds but contains mustangs as well.

Managed by the California BLM, but located in Nevada, is the **High Rock HMA**, containing 115,000 acres located approximately 46 miles north of Gerlach. Spanish-type mustangs and palomino pintos live here. Also managed by the California BLM is **Fox Hog HMA** with 119,000 acres in the Granite Range north of Gerlach. (Three other HMAs are nearby— half in California and half in Nevada—managed by the California BMA. **Twin Peaks HMA** is connected at the top to smaller **Buckhorn** and **Coppersmith HMAs**, which are all described in the California chapter. For maps of each of these HMAs, see the California chapter.)

A popular and accessible Nevada mustang-viewing area is **Calico Mountains/Leadville Canyon HMA**. Follow Highway 447 north through Gerlach. On the north side of Gerlach, take Highway 34 to the right. Eventually highway 34 turns to gravel just over 20 miles from town. If you keep following the road another 7 to 8 miles, you will come to the mouth of Leadville Canyon. From the mouth to the top of the canyon and just beyond, is the area where horses can be spotted at relatively close range.

Nevada's Interstate 80 passes near and through many HMAs. A large group of these is situated on approximately 1.5 million acres located between Sparks and Lovelock, and includes **Blue Wing Mountain, Shawave Mountain, Nightengale,** and **Seven Troughs HMAs.** Many dirt roads lead into this area north of Interstate 80. It is possible to access the HMAs from roads leading north through Imlay (going over Imlay Summit), through Lovelock via Highway 399, and directly off Highway 80 taking the Toulon Exit north, or the Nightingale Exit north. All of these routes, including Highway 399, become gravel or dirt roads eventually. You can also get to these HMAs from Winnemucca, taking the Jungo Road—a well-traveled dirt road. There is also limited access from Highway 447 on the west. Since this area is so huge, and there are so many interconnecting dirt roads, it is easy to get lost. Anyone wishing to view horses should first stop at the BLM office in Reno to obtain a topographical map and advice about the area.

A grey and a grey sabino gelding await adoption at the Wild Horse and Burro Show in Reno, Nevada.

West Central

One of best places to see many mustangs up close is the **Palomino Valley Adoption and Holding Facility** near Sparks. Take State Highway 445 (off Interstate 80 at Sparks) north toward Pyramid Lake. After about 15 miles you will see the brown wooden BLM sign on the right. This is the largest holding facility in the U.S. where thousands of gathered horses are brought for inspection, identification, veterinary treatment, and adoption. You can see different sizes, shapes and colors of mustangs as well as watch their behavior. Genders are kept in separate huge pens and are fascinating to watch as they run and interact. During the spring and summer it is especially enjoyable to watch the new foals playing together. The office is open weekdays from 8-5. Even when the inside office is closed, you can still drive or walk around the perimeter to see the horses. If you are patient, a wild horse may approach you through the fence. Since you might be the first human these horses have ever approached, *please* make this experience a good one!

Many other HMAs are contained in this section of Nevada including the Carson City District HMAs: **Dogskin Mountain**, **Pinenut Mountain**, **Amargosa Valley**, and **Fish Springs HMA**. Wild horses are sometimes seen eating and resting at dawn on front lawns in residential subdivisions in the Carson Valley.

The **Virginia Range Protection Agency (VRWPA)** manages a state-owned area containing wild horse herds north of Virginia City, NV. "Comstock" horses are available for adoption at their facility at the same price as BLM horses, which includes gelding and freeze branding.

Central

On Highway 50 between Austin and Fallon, the **Desatoya HMA** crosses the highway between Austin and Cold Springs, but most of this smaller HMA is south of the highway in the Desatoya Mountains. **Clan Alpine HMA** is north of Highway 50, all the way from the New Pass Summit to the turnoff for Highway 121. Look for dirt roads leading north to access the horses. The Clan Alpine Mountain Range is included within its boundaries.

An easily-accessible HMA is the **North Stillwater HMA** found off Interstate 80 from the Coal Canyon Exit leading into West Humboldt Range to the southeast I80. There are usually over 100 horses clustered in one area just west of Big Ben Canyon in the North Stillwater Range.

Highway 50 contains some very large HMAs. **Fish Creek HMA** (275,000 acres) lies between Eureka and Austin. Approximately 50 miles east of Austin, you will see a sign that says Antelope Valley Road. Do not

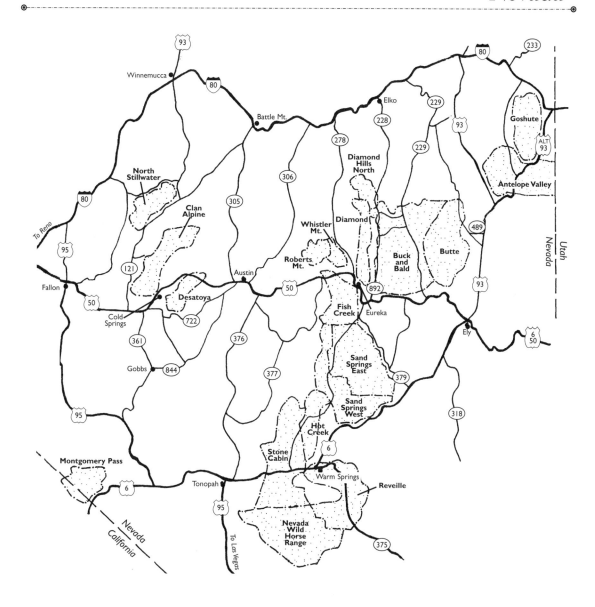

turn here, but continue 2.5 miles past this sign, and turn left on a dirt road. Approximately four miles down this valley road, which should afford you some herd watching, another road to the left leads into Brown's Canyon, another spot for horse watching. (Only 125 horses remain in this area due to gathers brought on by drought conditions, however.) This is a historic area for curly horses. The imported Lokai Curly breed (mistakenly called Bashkir Curly) was brought from Russia into this range in 1874 by a local horse breeder. Curly horses are still found here in mustang herds. Curly-coated horses have been found to be hypo-allergenic like poodles!

Continuing east on Highway 50 you will pass to the south of many other HMAs such as **Roberts Mountain**, **Whistler**, **Diamond**, and **Buck and Bald**. These HMAs are smaller and not as easily visited.

Southern

Heading south on Highway 95 out of Tonopah, many bands of horses can be spotted on the west side of the road. A bladed dirt road on the right side of the highway approximately 3 miles south of Tonopah leads to Alkali Springs. The road is suitable for cars. At the end of the road, turn right onto a paved road that will lead back to Highway 95. Several bands of horses live along this 10-mile stretch, including several appaloosa stallions. The horses are accustomed to traffic and can provide some excellent photos. Burros are often seen north and south of Goldfield and around the town of Beatty.

On Highway 6 east of Tonapah and west of Warm Springs lies the BLM's **Stone Cabin HMA** (with smaller, adjoining **Reveille** and **Hot Creek HMAs**) on both sides of the road. The first BLM gather was held here. "Stone Cabin Greys" were popular large mustangs (due to Percheron introduction) in earlier days. Contributing to the general population are the 600 or so wild horses on the 400,000-acre **Nevada Wild Horse Preserve** (established in 1962 as the first wild horse range in the U.S.) on Nellis Air Force Bombing and Gunnery Range due south (most of which is closed to the public).

Continuing to the east on Highway 6 past Warm Springs, you will drive through **Sand Springs HMA**. These horses have been known to cross the highway to find water, so take care and drive slowly!

Also near Highway 6 but straddling the California border is **Montgomery Pass HMA**. It is managed by the California BLM (see California chapter).

Eastern

Antelope Valley HMA and **Goshutes HMA** are right next to the Utah border. Off Alternate Highway 93 to the southeast, dirt roads lead to this wild horse area.

Mustangs often possess superior stamina and endurance. It is easy to see why as these bays traverse steep hillsides to reach water in Nightengale Mountain HMA.

Mustang with curly-coated ancestry gathered at Stone Cabin HMA in Nevada. This one's color is red chestnut with a white star.

Nevada

For more Nevada Wild Horse and Burro information contact:

BLM National Wild Horse and Burro Team (Nevada):
(800) 417-9647

BLM Nevada State Office
1340 Financial Blvd.
PO Box 12000
Reno, NV 89520
(775) 861-6400
www.nv.blm.gov

BLM Palomino Valley Holding Facility: (775) 475-2222

BLM Battle Mountain Field Office (Fish Creek, Roberts
   Mt./Whistler, Diamond HMAs)
50 Bastian Road
Battle Mountain, NV 89820-2332
(775) 635-4000

BLM Carson City Field Office (Clan Alpine HMA)
5665 Morgan Mill Road
Carson City, NV 89701-1448
(775) 885-6000

BLM Elko Field Office (Maverick-Medicine, Rock Creek
   HMAs)
3900 Idaho Street
Elko, NV 89801
(775) 753-0200

BLM Ely Field Office (Antelope Valley, Buck and Bald,
   Goshutes HMAs)
702 North Industrial Way
Ely, NV 89301
(775) 289-1800

BLM Las Vegas District Field Office (Nevada Wild Horse
   Range)
4765 W. Vegas Drive
Las Vegas, NV 89108-2135
(702) 647-5024

BLM Surprise Field Office (Buckhorn, Coppersmith, Fox Hog,
   High Rock HMAs)
602 Cressler Street
Cedarville, CA 96104
(530) 279-6101

BLM Tonopah Field Office (Stone Cabin, Reveille, Hot Creek
   HMAs)
1553 S. Main Street
Tonopah, NV 89049-0911
(775) 482-7800

BLM Winnemucca Field Office (Sahwave Mt., Bluewing,
   Nightengale, Seven Troughs HMAs)
5100 E. Winnemucca Blvd.
Winnemucca, NV 89445
(775) 623-1500

State of Nevada Commission for the Preservation of Wild
   Horses: www.state.nv.us/cnr/horse01.htm

National Wild Horse and Burro Show Association (annual
   show in Reno, NV, BLM, wild horse and burro promotion
   and information. htt://wild-horse.org

Reno Wild Horse Association (prison training, protection,
   promotion, and preserving the wild horses of America)
   email: NWHA@kozmail.com

Virginia Range Wildlife Protection Association (VRWPA)
   (775) 741-0180; www.vrwpa.org

Wild Horse Organized Assistance (WHOA)
   (775) 851-4817

Wild Horse Spirit, Ltd.
   (775) 329-0992; www.wildhorsespirit.org

To volunteer:
Contact your nearest District Field Office, or contact: BLM
Palomino Valley Holding Facility: (775) 475-2222 (Sparks,
NV) or email: skipping@nv.blm.gov

New Mexico

Most of the mustangs in the U.S. today descend from Spanish horses first brought to New Mexico to horse breeding ranches near Santa Fe. Juan de Onate, a Spanish colonizer, herded 25 stallions, 55 mares, and an unknown number of foals onto a hacienda in 1598 — and then later brought 800 more!

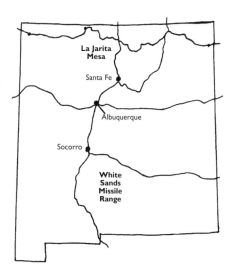

Escapees and those stolen or set loose spread in all directions to establish most of the great wild horse herds, and provided horses for the Native American tribes. Today, New Mexico has only a few wild horses and ranges left.

Northern

Highway 64, which goes from the Four Corners area of Shiprock to Clayton at the Oklahoma border, can provide some memorable wild horse encounters. Besides lots of Navajo horses grazing in front of pink cliffs under endless blue horizons (see the Arizona chapter) there exist several small, wild bands on Forest Service land west of Dulce, NM.

About 20 miles west of Dulce, in the **Carson National Forest**, turn north off Highway 64 onto the dirt road at a small, brown sign reading "Forest Road 310." Follow the signs up the mountain to **Cabresto Canyon** turn off, and go down the other side (not recommended in winter or early spring due to mud or snow). You will end up in a pleasant valley shared by oil and gas pumping stations (watch for large trucks) and wild horses. Despite the busy setting (or maybe because of it) you may round a bend in the road and come face to face with a wild band! Follow the signs to **Ulibarri Canyon** to find the pinto herd grazing in a meadow on the left side of the road. When you go back out of the canyons to Highway 64, you may see some wild horses grazing on either side of the road for a couple of miles as you head wast toward Dulce.

New Mexico

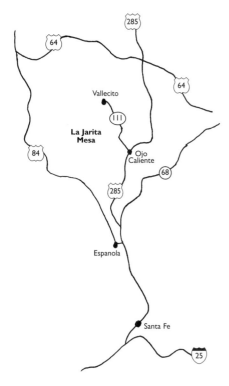

Santa Fe, NM, used to be the home of a prison wild horse training program at a facility just south of town on Highway 14. The prison is still there, but the attractive adobe and black wrought-iron corrals now stand empty. Hopefully, trained mustangs will be available for adoption here again.

The **Calle del Rio** herd is in an area near Santa Fe that is very hard to access by vehicle off Airport Road on Highway 62. At last count there were only 17 horses.

La Jarita Mesa is located near the town of Ojo Caliente north of Espanola (and Santa Fe) on Highway 285. This heavily-forested area has a small herd of horses on the mountain top. These horses can be seen (sometimes) by taking the horseback trip offered by the folks at **Vallecitos Stables** in nearby Vallecito, NM.

Central

In Albuquerque, the Bernalillo County Sheriff's Posse Arena hosts BLM adoptions usually in May or June. About 100 horses, burros, and demonstrations by local mustang owners are featured.

The BLM's **Bordo Atravesado Wild Horse Area** lies east of Socorro, NM. Take U.S. 380 12 miles east from San Antonio, NM (which is a few miles south of Socorro), then turn north onto County Road 2112 and go 9 miles, turning east and continuing for about 4 miles to the southwestern boundary of the HMA. The first wild horses here (2 mares and a stallion) reportedly wandered in from the Bosque del Apache Wildlife Refuge in the early 1950s. The population here has ranged from a low of 25 in 1971 to a high of 69 in 1985. Fifty horses are the average. The northern portion of this area, comprising 7,000 acres, has important scenic qualities and has been designated as the Stallion Wilderness Study Area.

Southern

White Sands Missile Range (which is closed to the public) was a refuge to wild horses with a rare pacing gene from 1940 to 1994. In 1994, a drought dried up the food and water supply. The military gathered most of the 1,800 horses at that time, and in 1999 the remaining 70 horses were transported to a private sanctuary in South Dakota by the **International Society for the Protection of Mustangs and Burros (ISPMB)**. See the South Dakota listing for more information on the ISPMB.

A pinto stallion (center) and his band of colorful look-alikes and others in Ulibarri Canyon on Forest Service land near Dulce, New Mexico.

For more New Mexico Wild Horse and Burro information contact:
BLM New Mexico State Office
1474 Rodeo Road
PO Box 27115
Santa Fe, NM 87502-0115
(505) 438-7400
www.nm.blm.gov

BLM Texas, Oklahoma, New Mexico Resource Office:
1-800-237-3642

BLM Socorro Field Office (Bordo Atravesado Wild Horse Area)
198 Neel Ave. NW
Socorro, NM 87801-4648
(505) 835-0412

U.S. Forest Service (Carson National Forest)
(505) 753-7331

BLM and Forest Service information and gift shop (Santa Fe): (505) 438-7542; www.publiclandsinfo.org

New Mexico Horse Project (website featuring information and DNA testing of NM mustangs): www.nmhp.org

Vallecitos Stables, near Santa Fe, NM (505) 753-7331 (La Jarita Mesa wild horse trips)

To volunteer:
BLM New Mexico, Oklahoma, and Texas Resource Office:
1-800-237-3642;
email: dharring@nm0151wp.nmso.nm.blm.gov

North Carolina

Cape Lookout National Seashore's Shackleford Banks' diminutive "Banker Ponies" descended from stock that swam to the nearest land from shipwrecked Spanish Galleons 300 years ago. Today they graze in easily-spotted family groups or bachelor bands among the dunes and in the maritime forests on this 10-mile long island, and on smaller Carrot Island.

With motorized vehicles prohibited, Shackleford Island is a popular spot for picnics, wind surfing, boating, shell collecting—and horse watching! Protected and managed by a local non-profit organization called The Foundation for Shackleford Horses, and the National Park Service, these horses tolerate close proximity by visitors and picture-takers, but please don't touch! The herds have their own U.S. Congressional Protection Act, set forth in 1997, which stipulates their population will number "not less than 100 horses and not more than 110." This is important to maintain a viable genetic pool. The ferry from Beaufort, NC, to Shackleford Island costs about $15 a person.

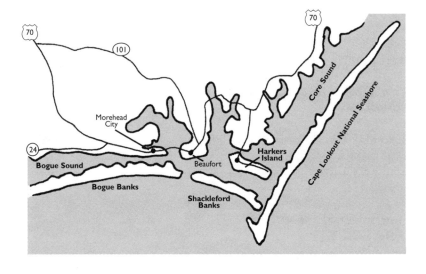

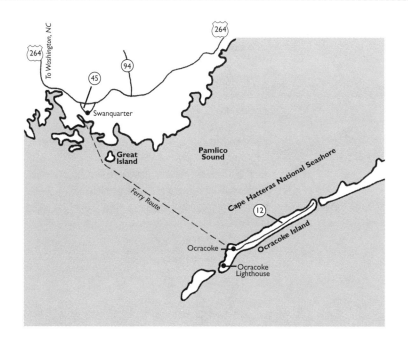

Another 42 wild horses (probably relatives of the Shackleford bunch) roam Carrot Island, which is between Shackleford and Beaufort—also accessible by Beaufort ferries.

North of Shackleford, in the **Cape Hatteras National Seashore**, more wild horses are found on **Ocracoke Island**, accessible by toll ferry from Swanquarter off Highway 264 east of Washington. Due to unfortunate horse- vehicle accidents, the horses are now restricted to a fenced enclosure for public viewing.

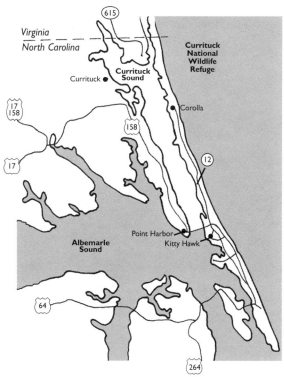

Farther north up the coast, near the border of North Carolina and Virginia, the **Currituck National Wildlife Refuge** is located on the north end of **Corolla Island**, a few miles from the Currituck Beach Lighthouse. Here endangered plants, wild boar, and Corolla's wild horses have a safe 1,800-acre haven. People may enter the refuge on foot or via 4-wheel drive vehicles over a cattle guard.

Where the
Wild Ones Roam

North Carolina

For more North Carolina Wild Horse and Burro information contact:
BLM Eastern States Office
7450 Boston Boulevard
Springfield, VA 22153
(703) 440-1600
www.blm.gov/eso

Cape Hatteras National Seashore: (252) 473-2111
(Okracoke Island)

Cape Lookout National Seashore: (252) 728-2250
(Shackleford Island and Carrot Island)
www.nps.gov/calo.hrs.htm

Corolla Wild Horse Fund: (252) 45308152
www.corollawildhorses.com

The Foundation for Shackleford Horses
P.O. Box 181
Beaufort, NC 28516
(919) 225-1181
www.shacklefordhorses.org

North Carolina Wild Horse Association-NCWHA (support and
education for mustang and burro adopters)
Mocksville, NC
(336) 940-2044
www.ncwildhorse.com

*"Ariel," a flaxen chestnut-colored
filly with a white star from
Shackleford Island, NC, where all
the "Banker Ponies" have names!*

North Dakota

When the Park Service established Theodore Roosevelt National Park in the Little Missouri Badlands of southwest North Dakota in the mid-1900s, a herd of original Spanish mustangs was inadvertently trapped within its boundaries.

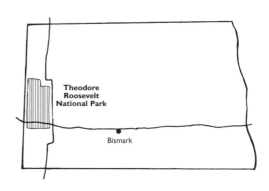

During the 1980s, the National Park Service introduced larger, purebred quarter horse and Arabian stallions. The original Spanish mustangs were purchased by brothers Frank and Leo Kuntz, who established a conservancy to continue the breed. The horses were found to have descended from Native American Chief Sitting Bull's herds taken after his surrender, and were called "Nokota Horses." Designated the "honorary state equine" in 1993, a small demonstration herd of Nokota Horses has been placed back in Theodore Roosevelt National Park, and can be visited on Interstate 94 near Medora, ND.

For more North Dakota Wild Horse and Burro information contact:
BLM Montana State Office (includes North and South Dakota)
5001 Southgate Drive
Billings, MT 59107-6800
(406) 896-5004
www.mt.blm.gov

U.S. Forest Service/Theodore Roosevelt National Park:
   (701) 623-4466; www.nps.gov/thro

The Nokota Horse Conservancy: (701) 782-4323 www.nokotahorse.org

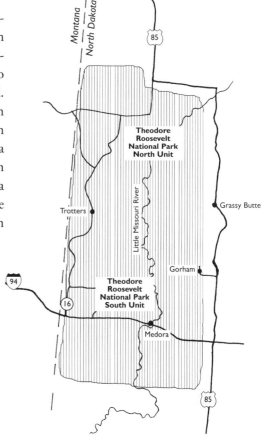

Oklahoma

If you can't make it all the way to the West to view or adopt wild horses, Oklahoma has three facilities that would be happy to help you out.

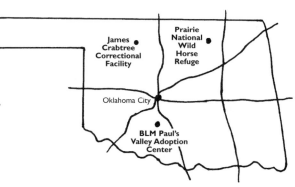

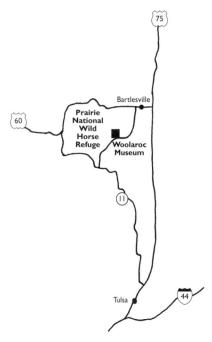

Northeastern

Bartlesville, OK, is home to 1,570 mustangs on 18,000 acres in the federally-funded **Prairie National Wild Horse Refuge**. Privately-owned Woolarac Museum adjoins this sanctuary, which is off Highway 75 approximately 50 miles north of Tulsa on Highway 123 south of Bartlesville.

Central

The BLM **Paul's Valley Adoption and Holding Facility** holds silent-bid adoptions the second Tuesday of each month from May to October. The facility is south of

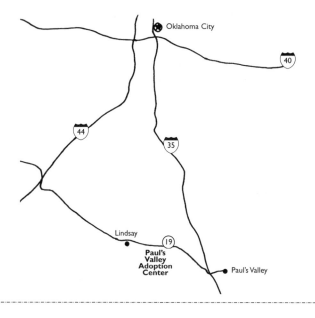

Oklahoma City and north of Pauls Valley. Take State Highway 19 west from Interstate 35 at Paul's Valley. Call ahead before visiting. Mustangs transported here from Nevada and other western states are offered at other locations around Oklahoma — call for the adoption schedule.

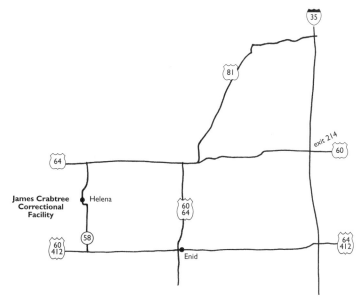

Approved adopters can choose a BLM mustang from the **James Crabtree Correctional Center** in Helena, OK. During the spring and summer months, you can also have your wild horse trained for a per-day fee. Training takes up to 90 days. The facility can train 23 horses at a time, so there may be a waiting list. Helena is located approximately 50 miles west of Interstate 35. Take Highway 60 west (exit 214) off of I35 to Highway 64 west, then take Highway 58 south to Helena.

For more Oklahoma BLM Wild Horse and Burro information contact:
BLM New Mexico State Office (includes Oklahoma and Texas)
1474 Rodeo Road
PO Box 27115
Santa Fe, NM 87502-0115
(505) 438-7400
www.nm.blm.gov

BLM Moore Field Station
221 N. Service Road
Moore, OK 73160-4946
(405) 794-9624

Prairie National Wild Horse Refuge (Bartlesville, OK):
(918) 333-5575

BLM Tulsa Field Station
7906 E. 33rd Street, Ste 101
Tulsa, OK 74145-1352
(918) 621-4100

BLM Pauls Valley Adoption and Holding Facility
(800) 237-3642

James Crabtree Correctional Facility (Helena, OK):
(580) 852-3221

To volunteer:
(800) 237-3642
email: dharring@nm.blm.gov

Oregon

In the 1880s, feral Spanish horses from California banded with escapees from the Gold Rush miners and produced large wild horse herds in Oregon. By 1928, an estimated 10,000 mustangs roamed the southeastern Oregon deserts.

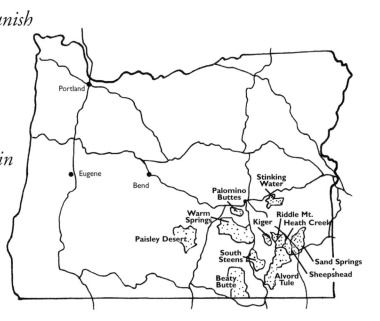

Their numbers declined until 1971 when the BLM was assigned to protect them. At that time, the BLM was alerted by local citizens of an isolated band of zebra dun horses in the Beaty Butte area of southeast Oregon. After genetic testing proved they were original Spanish type, the BLM moved the herd to two protected locations in the Kiger Gorge and Riddle Mountain areas, and called them "Kiger Mustangs." Today, the Oregon BLM still manages the Kigers carefully, and wild horse herds of appaloosas, palominos, drafthorses, pintos and others in the HMAs in Oregon. Contact the Burns District office before visiting the herds for up-to-date road conditions.

Southeastern

The **Kiger HMA** contains 37,000 acres and 50 to 80 horses. To view these unusual, predominately zebra dun-colored mustangs (brownish-yellow with blackish-brown stripes down the back, on legs, sometimes across the back, and black ear tips and rims), you must drive 10 miles on a very rocky, narrow dirt road (make sure you carry a spare tire or two). During snowy or wet seasons, this road is not accessible by vehicle. Off Highway 205 (south of Burns, and north of Frenchglen) exit at the Diamond turnoff. Follow the road heading to Diamond, pass through the tiny town, and when you have gone 16 miles from Hwy. 205, look for an unmarked, good dirt road heading to the right. A short way up this road you will see a sign that identifies the road leading to the Kiger viewing area 8.5 miles farther. Continue climbing up the road, and when you reach the viewing area, park and walk the short distance to the lookout point. Below and to the left is a hidden stream, and you can see the Kiger mustangs as they water and graze, run across the valley below, and disappear over the rocky hills in front of you. Bring binoculars for the best view of the stripes!

Riddle Mountain HMA is a nearby, smaller HMA that also contains Kiger Mustangs, but it is remote and inaccessible by vehicle.

The most easily-viewed group of Oregon mustangs are the large pintos that live in the **South Steens Mountain HMA**. During the day, horses can be watched as they graze and rest in this 250,000-acre range near the intersection of South Loop Road and Highway 205, (north of Fields, south of Frenchglen), on or close to the road up the first couple of miles of the gravel South Loop Road, and in the nearby sagebrush-covered hills. If you park

Herds of large, muscular pinto mustangs grace the hills of South Steens Mountain HMA in Oregon.

and walk up the hillsides, you can come across family groups quietly grazing unseen in the folds of the grassy mesas. Wild horses can also be found on the tops of the steep, rocky slopes overlooking Highway 205 before Roaring Springs Ranch. The lava rock stones are sharp, and in the summer there are rattlesnakes—bring plenty of water, and wear hiking boots and long pants. On Highway 205 just north of Roaring Springs Ranch you will see large stud piles of manure on the highway as horses often come down for water right next to the road. If you drive through this area at night, drive slowly as there have been collisions. (A "Wild Horse Crossing" sign here would be a good idea.)

Other HMAs such as **Alvord/Tule, Coyote Lake, Jackie's Butte, Three Fingers,** and **Pokegama** are found clustered in the southeast corner of Oregon or along its southern border, with commingling herds occurring in the adjacent California, Idaho, and Nevada deserts, plains and mountainous areas.

South Central

Burns Wild Horse Adoption and Holding Facility is located south of Burns (in Hines, OR) on Highway 20. The public is welcome 8-4 on weekdays, and tours can be arranged by request.

Traveling west between Burns and Bend on Hwy 20 will take you past **Palomino Butte HMA** (containing only palominos, of course) on the south side of the road. The HMA is in an area inaccessible to vehicles because of rough terrain, however. Similar bad road conditions prevent public access to other specialized HMAs such as **Stinking Water** (managed for drafthorse herds) and **Warm Springs** (appaloosa herds). Mustangs gathered from all Oregon herds are available at the Burns Corrals, so give them a call to see what horses are available for adoption.

For more Oregon Wild Horse and Burro information contact:
BLM Burns District Office (Burns Holding and Adoption Facility)
HC 74
12533 Hwy. 20 West
Hines, OR 97738
(541) 573-4400
www.or.blm.gov/Burns/Horseburro/horse.html

Pacific Wild Horse Club (promotes and protects mustangs and burros): www.pacificwildhorseclub.org

Frenchglen Hotel (Frenchglen, OR): (541) 493-2825
(lodging and wild horse information and gifts)

Steens Mountain Resort (Frenchglen, OR): (800) 542-3765
(lodging and wild horse information and gifts.)

To volunteer:
BLM Burns District Office: (541) 573-4400
email: dbolstad@or.blm.gov

Zebra dun-colored "Kiger Mustang" weanlings show uniformity in color and characteristics (such as leg and dorsal stripes, hooked black-tipped ears, large eyes, and delicate muzzles) of this special herd from Kiger and Riddle Mountain HMAs.

South Dakota

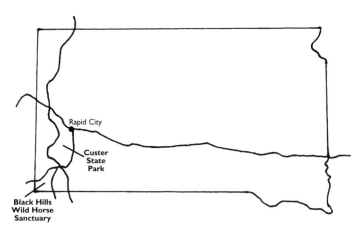

The **Black Hills Wild Horse Sanctuary** is privately run by the Institute of Range Management (IRAM). They offer 2-hour bus tours departing three times daily to observe mustangs on this 11,000-acre prairie heaven for un-adoptable BLM horses. Open Monday through Saturday, Memorial Day to Labor Day, it is on State Highway 71 (south of Rapid City and Hot Springs). Turn right just past the Cheyenne River Bridge near Cascade Falls. You can volunteer, sponsor a mustang, or adopt a colt. Call ahead for times and prices of tours and chuck wagon cookouts.

The **International Society for the Protection of Mustangs and Burros (ISPMB)** plans to open an ecotourism center on the Pine Ridge Indian Reservation in the south-western part of the state. Watch for its opening!

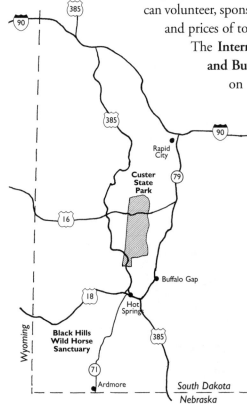

For more South Dakota Wild Horse and Burro information contact:
Black Hills Wild Horse Sanctuary/IRAM
PO Box 998
Hot Springs, SD 57747
(605) 745-5955; www.wildmustangs.com

International Society for the Protection of Mustangs and Burros (ISPMB)
HCR 73, Box 7C
Interior, SD 57750-9606
(605) 433-5600; www.ispmb.org

BLM Montana/Dakotas State Office
5001 Southgate Dr.
Billings, MT 59107-6800
(406) 896-5004; www.mt.blm.gov

Tennessee

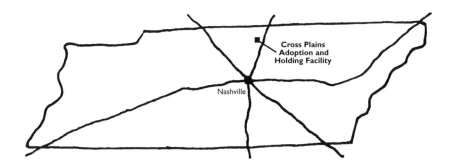

The **BLM Cross Plains Adoption and Holding Facility** brings Western wild horses and burros to eastern states' adopters! Located 35 miles north of Nashville off Hwy. 65 onto Highway 25 West (Exit 112), it's open year-round. Call for visiting hours and adoption information.

For more Tennessee Wild Horse and Burro information contact:
BLM Jackson Field Office
411 Briarwood Dr., Ste. 404
Jackson, MS 30206
(601) 977-5400

Cross Plains Wild Horse and Burro Adoption Center:
(615) 654-2180

Middle Tennessee Mustang Association:
(615) 793-3776

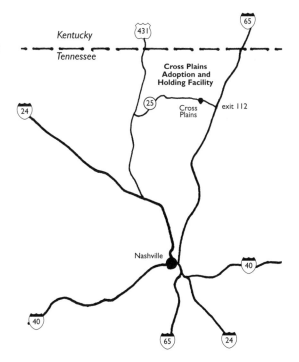

Texas

Despite the fact that Texas was once the largest mustang range in the nation, there are no BLM or Forest Service public lands for them to roam in the entire state today.

Texas has a grand wild horse history, however, including early American explorer Zebulon Pike's discovery that huge herds of free-roaming wild horses were a hazard to travelers. Advance scouts had to chase away the large wild horse herds as settlers' horses often tried to join them, despite every effort to stop them. Sometimes mistaken for large mounted war parties of Indians, mustangs regularly inspected prairie-crossers' wagons, horses, and livestock from overlooking hills. Legend tells how wild horse bands "spirited away" as many as 700 domestic horses at a time, and not one was ever recovered. Today, a large number of Texas residents have adopted American mustangs and burros and "returned" them to this area. There are many active Texas mustang groups, organized shows, and sales. Glen Rose, TX, was the site of the BLM's 1998 4th Annual Regional Wild Horse and Burro Show, and the BLM brings wild horses and burros regularly to Texas for adoptions.

For more Texas Wild Horse and Burro information contact:
BLM New Mexico State Office (includes Oklahoma and Texas)
1474 Rodeo Road
PO Box 27115
Santa Fe, NM 87502-0115
(505) 438-7400/800-237-3642
www.nm.blm.gov

American Indian Horse Registry - AIHR (club, registry which accepts BLM mustangs, holds annual shows and events in Texas)
(512) 398-6642; www.aihr.freeyellow.com

Black Beauty Ranch (private sanctuary for rescued BLM or National Park Service burros; offers burros for adoption)
P.O. Box 367
Murchison, TX 75778
(903) 469-3811
www.blackbeautyranch.org

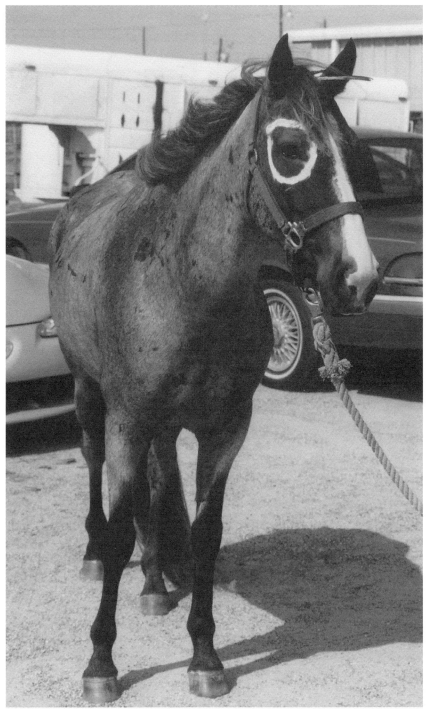

Spanish Mustang "Fandango Mist" has a traditional circle painted around his eye. He was a part of the 1999 American Indian Horse Show in Corsicana, Texas.

Utah

Southern Utah had more than 15,000 wild horses roaming freely in the 1920s! Today, this state contains quite a few HMAs and a roomy adoption and holding facility. Contact the Salt Lake City BLM office before visiting the herds for up-to-date road conditions.

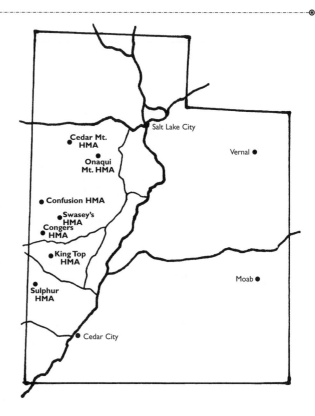

Southwestern

The **Sulphur HMA**, located in the Needle Mountain Range, contains original Spanish-type mustangs common to only a few other isolated areas in the U.S. Zebra duns, grullos and grullas (grullos are male; grullas are female) are common here. Look for "sooty face" or nose-bridge darkness, front and back leg stripes, chest stripes, stripes along the back both vertically and horizontally, and black-rimmed ears. 225 horses were counted here in 1996. This protected area is hard to access, however. Rough dirt roads make high-clearance, 4-wheel drive vehicles mandatory. Horses migrate to higher elevations during the heat of summer, but can be found on the hills of Hamlin and Pine Valley in late fall and spring. Most wild horses are seen in the Mountain Home and Indian Peak portions of the range. Take State Highway 21, and approximately 45 miles west of Milford look for the BLM sign reading "Pots Sum Pa." Turn south on this road to enter the northeastern part of Sulphur HMA.

Central

Conger Mountain HMA is located 75 miles west of Delta, Utah. Common colors in this herd are black, roan, palomino and dun. Horses are on the small side, and the herd numbers 60 to 100. Travel west from Delta on State

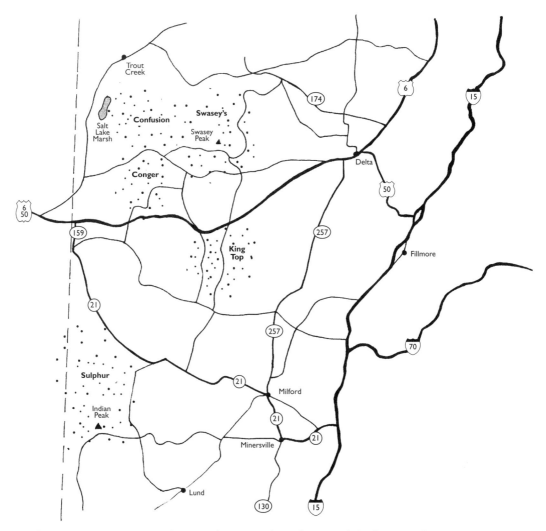

Highway 50/6 approximately 75 miles to Little Valley Road (milepost 16). Turn north on Little Valley Road and travel approximately 8 miles to the Skunk Springs (Camp Canyon) Road. Horses can usually be found in the vicinity of Conger Springs, Camp Canyon and Skunk Springs. Another mustang viewing spot is farther west on Highway 50/6. To reach this area, go north at the Elksdale turnoff near milepost 8. Proceed about 15 miles to the intersection of Knoll Springs and Old Highway 50/6. Horses can be seen on the slopes east of Knoll Springs and south of Cowboy Pass.

King Top HMA is located south of Conger Mt. HMA, but in the same general area. Travel west from Delta on State Highway 50/6 approximately 75 miles to milepost 16 at the Little Valley Road intersection. Go south at the intersection and travel 6 miles to Ferguson Desert Road. Turn east onto

Ferguson Desert Road and travel for 12 miles to the turnoff to Probst Pond (commonly known as Snake Pass Road). Go east on Snake Pass Road and look for horses anywhere north or south of the road for the next 8 miles. Another good area to view King Top horses, particularly during the summer early or late in the day, is in the vicinity of Eck's Knoll Reservoir. This reservoir is reached by continuing south from the Probst Pond sign on Ferguson Desert Road another 3 miles. At the fork in the road, take the left-hand fork and travel 1.5 miles to Eck's Knoll. Stop when in view of the reservoir and scan the basin for horses. Black, bay, and brown colors predominate.

The **Confusion HMA** has a large number of gray and light-colored horses that are taller and heavier than usual due to Percheron introduction in the past. This herd is managed to preserve the color and size of these horses. Travel west from Delta, Utah, on Highway 50/6 approximately 90 miles to the Utah/Nevada border. Turn north at the road sign to Gandy. Travel approximately 12 miles to the intersection with Old Highway 50/6 at Robinson's Ranch. Turn east at the sign (through the ranch) and go approximately 6 miles to Knoll Springs. Horses can be viewed early or late in the day at the springs or in the foothills of the Conger Mountains to the southeast. Continue east up old Highway 50/6 approximately 5 more miles to the intersection of the Gandy/Foote's Ranch Road. Heading north toward the Gandy Salt Marsh Complex, horses are frequently seen along the benches and riparian areas between the road and the Confusion Mountains. The roads to Swasey Spring are maintained and traversable by passenger cars during dry weather. All other viewing areas of this HMA require high-clearance, 4-wheel drive vehicles.

Swasey Mountains HMA contains gray-colored horses also. Travel west from Delta on State Highway 50/6 approximately 30 miles to the signed turnoff to Antelope Spring and Long Ridge Reservoir. Turn north and travel approximately 30 miles to an intersection with a large, fenced pond south of the road. Horses can be found watering at this pond early or late in the day during the summer. Head east at the intersection toward Swasey Spring. Horses may be seen in the foothills and canyons along the east side of the Swasey Mountains.

Northwestern

The first HMA you will pass when traveling on I-80 west from Salt Lake City will be the **Onaqui Mountains HMA**. Take I-80 approximately 20 miles west to the Lakepoint/Tooele exit. Travel south on Highway 36 though Tooele and Stockton. Go west on Highway 199 through Rush Valley and

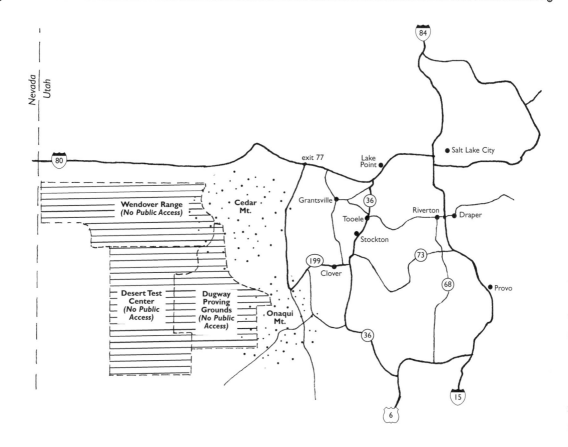

Johnson's Pass to Terra. Turn south at the BLM sign marked "Onaqui Mountains." Wild horses can be viewed along this road to Lookout Pass and the Pony Express Trail, and on the bench and flat areas along the east and west sides of the mountain range.

Cedar Mountain HMA is populated with predominately dark-colored cavalry remount ancestors, but other colors such as roan, gray, palomino and pinto are also found here. 270 horses were counted in 1996. To reach this HMA, take Interstate 80 west of Salt Lake City for 40 miles to the Dugway Road exit (Exit 77). Travel south approximately 17 miles to the Skull Valley Ranch. At the south end of the ranch, turn west at the BLM sign marked "Rydalch Pass—Eight Mile Spring." Go west about a mile to another BLM sign marked "Rydalch" and turn left. Travel across Skull Valley 14 miles to the Cedar Mountains. Horses can be viewed along the east or west side of the Cedars south to the **Dugway Proving Grounds'** (military installation that is closed to the public) boundary fence, and north to Hastings Pass. Do not enter the military area without permission.

North Central
South of Salt Lake City, off Interstate 15 on 68 South (take the Riverton/Draper Exit), is the **BLM Salt Lake City Regional Adoption and Holding Facility** in Butterfield Canyon. Although most adoptions are held in other parts of the state, some horses are available here. Call ahead before visiting.

This young stallion from Utah's Sulphur Herd has "Spanish Mustang" characteristics of hooked ears, short back, low-set tail, and lobo dun coloration.

For more Utah Wild Horse and Burro information contact:

BLM Law Enforcement Hotline to report abuse of Utah wild horses or burros: 1-800-722-3998

BLM Utah State Office
324 South State Street, Ste. 301
Salt Lake City, UT 84145-0155
(801) 539-4001
www.ut.blm.gov

BLM Cedar City Field Office (Sulphur HMA)
176 East D.L. Sargent Drive
Cedar City, UT 84720
(435) 586-2401

BLM Fillmore Field Office (Conger Mts. HMA, Confusion HMA, Swasey Mountains HMA, and King Top HMA)
35 E. 500 North
Fillmore, UT 84631
(435) 743-3100

BLM Salt Lake City Field Office (Onoqui Mt. HMA, Cedar Mt. HMA)
2370 South 2300 West
Salt Lake City, UT 84119
(801) 977-4300

BLM Salt Lake City Regional Adoption and Holding Facility
(801) 977-4300

Sulphur Springs Herd Mustang Registry: (208) 529-3074
http://business.fortunecity.com/mars/221/

To volunteer:
Salt Lake City Field Office: (801) 977-4300

This happy Utah resident adopted a pregnant roan mare and two weeks later became the owner of a bouncing, bald-faced baby colt!

Wyoming

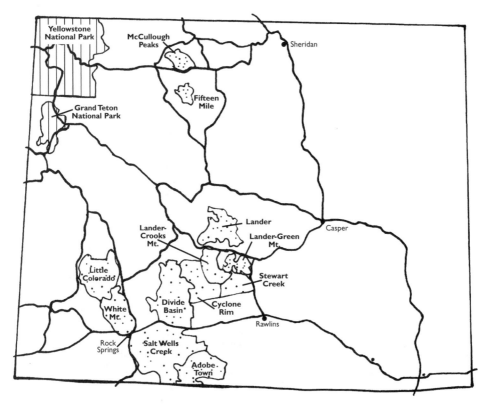

Southwestern

Wyoming contains a dozen or so large HMAs in the southwest portion of the state—roughly from west of Rawlins to east of Kemmerer. Beginning from the eastern side, **Lander-Green Mountain HMA** lies directly south and east of Jeffrey City off Highway 287. Whiskey Peak, el. 9215 ft., lies within this HMA. There are grand vistas of the Red Desert, Sweetwater Rocks, and the Oregon Trail. There are many other species of wildlife contained in this green, highly-vegetated HMA, including elk, antelope, and moose. Mustangs here are ancestors of escapees from ranchers, miners, early settlers, and the U.S. Cavalry.

    Stewart Creek HMA lies just south of Lander-Green Mountain. Horses can be found from Highway 789/287 between Rawlins and Lander near Muddy Gap Junction where Highway 220 cuts off to Casper (on the west and south side of the highway). **Lander-Crooks Mountain HMA, Cyclone**

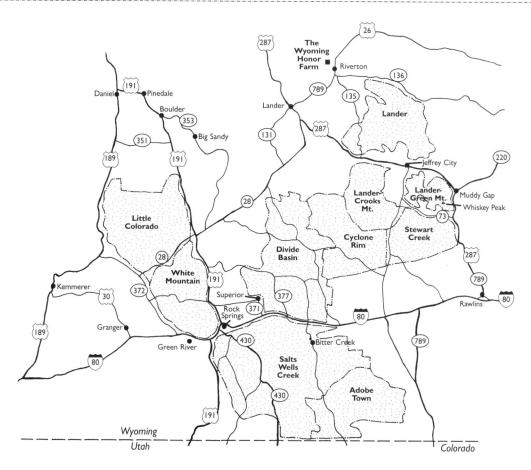

Rim HMA, and **Divide Basin HMA** abut Stewart Creek to the west. **Salt Wells Creek HMA** and **Adobe Town HMA** lie south of I-80 to the east of Highway 191 and the west of 789. North of I-80, between Highway 191 to the east and Highway 189 to the west, are **Little Colorado HMA** and **White Mountain HMA** (where you can find a petroglyph rock carving of an ancient Native American horse and rider). Drive north of Rock Springs along Highway 191 and look for wild horses on the west side of the road. Call the Wyoming District office for a specific HMA prior to visiting for up-to-date road conditions.

Central

The **Wyoming Honor Farm** prison in Riverton (just east of Lander on Highway 26) trains BLM mustangs and offers them for adoption to the public in the spring and fall. Using the "approach and retreat" method, they can train 100 horses at a time to be halter-trained, trailer-trained, and gentled.

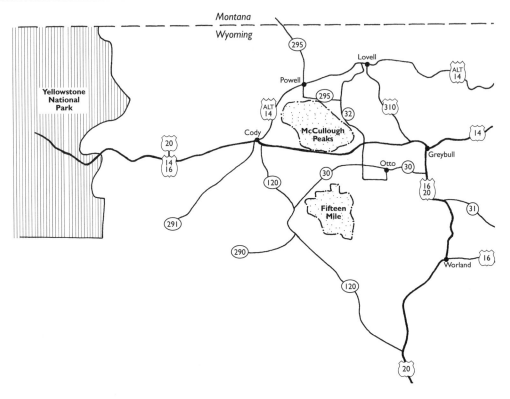

The Honor Farm has been gentling mustangs since 1988.

Lander HMA lies north of Jeffrey City above Highway 287 and west of Highway 135. This area contains about 177,000 acres of public land and includes grand vistas of the Copper, Owl Creek, and Wind River mountain ranges. In this same general location are three smaller HMAs: **Rock Creek**, **Conant Creek**, and **Dishpan Butte HMAs** that are south of Riverton and north of Highway 287, with mesas, rivers, rolling hills, and scenic views. Herds from these HMAs commingle, traveling back and forth freely between summer and winter pastures.

North Central

McCullough Peaks HMA and **Fifteen Mile HMA** are located north and south of Highway 14 between Cody and Greybull.

Northeast

The museum in Sundance, WY, off Interstate Highway 90 (close to the South Dakota/Wyoming border) has a display of the life of Bob Brislawn, who was famous for preserving the Spanish Mustang breed.

For more Wyoming Wild Horse and Burro information contact:
BLM Wyoming State Office
5353 Yellowstone Road
Cheyenne, WY 82003-1828
(307) 775-6256
www.wy.blm.gov

BLM Lander Field Office (Lander-Crooks HMA)
1335 Main Street
Lander, WY 82520-0589
(307) 332-8400

BLM Rock Springs Field Office (Salt Wells Creek, White Mountain, Little Colorado, Divide Basin, Adobe Town, Sweetwater HMAs)
280 Hwy. 191 North
Rock Springs, WY 82901-3448
(307) 352-0256

BLM Rawlins Field Office (Stewart Creek, Cyclone Rim HMAs)
1300 N. Third
Rawlins, WY 82301-2407
(307) 328-4200

BLM Wyoming Honor Farm (Riverton, WY): (307) 775-6097

Bighorn Canyon National Recreation Area Visitor Center
   (307) 548-2251

Pryor Mt. Mustang Association: (307) 775-6097

Pryor Mountain Wild Horse Refuge Webpage
   www.webcom.com/~ladyhawk/breeding.html

Two bay-colored mustangs find plenty of nourishment during the winter.

Other States

Other Northeastern and Midwestern States:
Connecticut, Delaware, District of Columbia, Illinois, Indiana, Iowa, Kansas, Maine, Maryland, Massachusetts, Michigan, Minnesota, Missouri, New Hampshire, New Jersey, New York, Ohio, Pennsylvania, Rhode Island, Vermont, West Virginia, and Wisconsin
> These states have BLM adoptions! Occasionally a wild horse herd is discovered, such as in the Ozark Mountains of Missouri.

For BLM Wild Horse and Burro adoption schedules and information contact:
BLM Milwaukee Field Office
310 West Wisconsin Ave., Ste. 450
Milwaukee, WI 53203
(414) 297-4400; (800) 293-1781

Danada (Wheaton, Illinois, wild horse project center): (630) 668-6012

Missouri Wild Horse League (protects Ozark wild horses)
PO Box 301
Eminence, MO 65466

BLM Wild Horse & Burro Toll-Free: 1-866-4mustangs

Other Southern States:
Alabama, Arkansas, Florida, Georgia, Kentucky, Louisiana, Mississippi, North and South Carolina, Tennessee, and Virginia.
> These states have some early mustang history. From the 1660s to 1750, Spanish "jennets" were bred in Florida, South Carolina, and Georgia. Some escaped into the wild. Also, in the late 1600s and early 1700s, Virginia tobacco farmers and Maryland legislators enacted laws restricting the large numbers of wild horses that roamed the swamps and fields. There still are a few feral horses in protected, wild areas today, such as the Ft. Polk Louisiana herds.

For BLM Wild Horse and Burro adoption schedules and information contact:
BLM Jackson Field Office
411 Briarwood Dr., Ste. 404
Jackson, MS 39206
(601) 977-5400; www.blm.gov/eso

BLM Eastern States Office Information Access Center
7450 Boston Blvd.
Springfield, VA 22153
(703) 440-1600

BLM Wild Horse & Burro Toll-Free: 1-866-4mustangs

Louisiana Wild Horses (adoptable wild horses roaming Ft. Polk Army training center)
(505) 282-5243; http://members.sonetcom.com/jimmy/lahorses/default.htm

South Florida Mustang Association: (561) 791-1755

Appendix

Mustang and Burro Organizations & Trainers

As the popularity of mustangs and burros grows, so do the number of registries, clubs, websites, trainers, and organizations specifically focusing on them. The information these people provide can be very helpful. There may also be an opportunity to engage in fun and educational activities with other mustang and burro owners. Sanctuaries and rescuers provide humane treatment in times of need, and wild horse and burro advocacy groups can lobby to change laws and bring awareness to animal rights isues.

However, when some individuals or groups become popular, their mission statement and original integrity are sometimes sacrificed for the thrill of having followers and money. Avoid supporting any organization or trainer who uses methods that are abusive or unsafe. Unfortunately, the general public will still flock to see wild animals "tamed" or "dominated" in the shortest possible time. If a method makes you uncomfortable, it is not the correct one to use. Report people to the BLM who are abusing BLM horses or burros. Let the organizers and the sponsors of the event know you won't support training methods and handling techniques that are disrespectful to the animals' safety or fear level. Don't rely on "magic" devices, workshops, tapes, or tack. Stay away from organizations that prohibit you from seeking advice or training from others, or censor any unfavorable response to their methods or events. Sometimes the best support systems are local friends holding small "events" or training sessions, or learning from a local trainer you know and respect.

This book attempts to help you recognize the methods, trainers, videos, and reading material that practice the philosophy of slow, quiet, gentle, horse psychology-based training that builds a dependable, trusting, solid horse over time. These methods work with all animals, they leave no "holes" in the training, and most importantly, they do no harm. It is possible to handle even aggressive or older animals using these techniques. Anything using excessive running in a round-pen, leg or head restraints, pain, snubbing, whips, force, or an emphasis on "submitting to human domination" are harmful physically and mentally, especially to wild animals that are already stressed by their new close proximity to man, and result in only fear-based compliance. These rougher techniques are mainly used for the promotional purposes of the human, or to provide a shortcut or quick fix. Correct gentling and training should be less of a "good show," and more like watching paint dry or grass grow, and the decisions the horse makes should be his or her own free choices. The tools used should give direction, not forced compliance.

It is not necessary to take your adopted horse across the country to a wild horse "expert" or special clinic. There is probably a humble, gentle, knowledgeable trainer in your community. Ask around until you find the right person if you are in need of help. Domestic horses that are bred in someone's fenced "back forty" and given minimal handling are sometimes harder to train than an adopted BLM mustang! If you make sure your mustang is at least well-gentled, there will be plenty of help in your community for boarding, veterinary treatment, hoof-care, training, shows, and inclusion into all regular equine activities.

A Word About Mustang Breed Registries

The definition of the mustang as a "breed" is a subject for debate. The question is whether a mustang is a breed with specific characteristics, or a mixed-breed horse in wild circumstances. Mustangs are now being created by breeding BLM mares and stallions in captivity. Are these offspring who will never run wild really mustangs, or does a mustang by definition of the word have to be born or bred feral?

Unlike other breeds whose color and body type is uniform, mustangs come in many colors and sizes, with sloping croups, rounded croups, round barrels, lean barrels, long backs, short backs, straight profiles, and "ram's heads." The difficulty of deciding what a "good" mustang should look like is complicated by the fact that most BLM mustangs are historically the result of heavier draft breeds and lighter riding breeds combined by man. Since the best breeding management seeks to equally match the size of both parents, mustangs may have disproportionate body parts, such as bigger feet or larger heads on smaller, leaner bodies. Ironically, the appearance of many mustangs is then judged harshly.

Whether or not a horse is registered really makes no difference if it is sound and well-trained, except for breeding purposes or entry into events or exclusive mention. Deliberately or accidentally allowing animals to breed always produces a certain number of unwanted and abused animals. It is not uncommon to see pictures of auction pens filled with hundreds of horses for sale, slaughter-bound truckloads of equines, or animals starving and neglected in disreputable breeders' yards. Breeding domestic mustangs will def-

Mustang and Burro Organizations

initely deprive some of the wild ones of adoptive homes. Registries may set impossible "standards" for the "breed" by which many mustangs will be judged negatively or rejected.

Registering a mustang is really done for the owner — a sense of pride, distinction, a nice certificate for the wall, perhaps a higher value, and if the club is local, activities to attend. Ideally, a mustang registry should accept any BLM mustang and not advocate breeding until there is a real shortage.

Since well-trained mustangs can and do participate successfully in general horse and rider activities, membership in a "mustang club" or "mustang registry" does not have to be the only activities you do with your mustang or burro. Clubs and registries can be a good way to connect with other owners and show off your animals. If there are enough adopters in your area, you might be able to put on a Mustang Appreciation Day and invite the press and public. If there is a local parade, ride or lead your wild horse through town. Be proud that you have an animal that has a long, rich history, and for your sake and the animal's, give them as much training as you can!

The following are organizations, registries, sanctuaries and clubs that specialize in mustangs. This book assumes no liability for your experiences or participation with them. They are as good as the people who run them, and people are only human. Keep your eyes and ears open, and enjoy your mustangs and burros!

American Curly Horse Association - ACHA
www.curlyhorse.web.com

American Donkey and Mule Society, Inc.
http://donkeys.com/ADMS.html
http://www.geocities.com/moredonkeys/

American Horse Protection Association, Inc. (AHPA)
(202) 965-0500

American Indian Horse Registry - AIHR (Registry, information, events)
www.indianhorse.com

American Wild Mustang Association - AWMA (Registry, information, events, breeding)
http://awmahr.nstmp.com

Bureau of Land Management, U.S. Government (BLM)
Nationwide Adoption Program
(866) 4MUSTANGS
www.adoptahorse.blm.gov

BLM Wild Horse and Burro National Office (National Wild Horse and Burro News)
www.wildhorseandburro.blm.gov

Colorado Horse Rescue
(303) 439-9217
Support and education for mustang and burro adopters.

Dancing Cloud Equine Rescue and Sanctuary (Rescue, training, and sanctuary for domestic, mustang, and native American horses)
Covelo, CA; (707) 983-6732

Forest Horse Webstore (Features books, videos, and training and care aids specifically geared toward gentling and training wild horses; uses gentled and trained BLM mustangs as models)
www.foresthorse.com

Foundation for Shackleford Horses
Beaufort, NC; (919) 225-1181
www.shacklefordhorses.org

The Fund for Animals
(307) 859-8840
Black Beauty Ranch website: www.blackbeautyranch.org

International Society for the Protection of Mustangs and Burros - ISPMB (Registry, sanctuary, adoptions, rescue, educational projects)
www.ispmb.com

KBR World of Wild Horses and Burros (News, information, events, training pages)
www.kbrhorse.net/whb

Lifesavers Wild Horse Rescue (Mustang and burro rescue and placement)
www.wildhorserescue.org

National Wild Horse and Burro show Association (annual Reno, NV, show, BLM wild horse and burro promotion and information) http://wild-horse.org

Nevada State Commission for the Preservation of Wild Horses/Mustang Manes and Tales Magazine (Quarterly magazine about wild horses in the U.S.; raises funds for wild horses and their habitat)
(775) 688-2626; www.state.nv.us/cnr/horse01.htm

North American Mustang Association and Registry (NAMAR) (Support and education for mustang and burro adopters; organizes horse shows, bi-monthly newsletter)
(972) 289-9344

North Carolina Wild Horse Association -NCWHA (Support and education for mustang and burro adopters - club located in NC)
www.ncwildhorse.com

Northwest Colorado Wild Horse Association (Support and education for mustang and burro adopters -club located in Colorado)
(970) 824-3868

Pacific Wild Horse Club (Support and education for mustang and burro adopters - club located in Oregon)
www.pacificwildhorseclub.org

Sorraia Mustang Studbook - SMS (Registry for Iberian-type mustangs, FAQ)
http://members.aol.com/oehorse/2

South Florida Mustang Association
(561) 791-1755

Virginia Range Wildlife Protection Association (Non-profit organization engaging in educational, scientific, developmental and range management activities on behalf of free-roaming horses; assistance to and adoptions of wild horses in Virginia City, NV area.)
(775) 881-2288
www.vrwpa.org

Wild Horse and Burro Freedom Alliance - WHBFA (Coalition of concerned equine animal welfare organizations)
www.savewildhorses.org

Wild Horse Hoofbeats Web Magazine (Stories and photos about herds, and interesting information written by adopters)
www.chaffee.net/~steague

Wild Horse Organized Assistance - WHOA (Support and education for mustang and burro adopters, care for orphaned foals, and assistance to wild, free-roaming horses - located in Nevada)
(775) 851-4817

For more organizations, contact the ones listed in this book and ask the members for further information on any other clubs or groups in your area!

Wild Horse and Burro Gentlers and Trainers

The following is a list of gentlers and trainers available for hire, and those who have produced books and videos for sale advocating horse psychology-based methods of handling wild horses. This does not mean people can't use a rope or a halter, a bit or a bridle, a saddle, a leg or a spur, or even a whip for use as a directional tool. Horses need clear, calm direction that is not pain- or fear-based. Only those who are capable of using aids and cues correctly and with the lightest precision should use them. I have made every effort to research and observe each trainer listed. (The exclusion of anyone is not an indication of the unsuitability of anyone's methods.) The book assumes no liability or responsibility for results or events occurring based on hiring these individuals or following their teachings. Choose only a gentler or trainer who will let you watch, visit, and ride under their supervision. Ask for references before hiring. If the trainer's barn is full, ask him or her for a referral to another trainer they recommend. With the help of wise, gentle, skilled horsemen and women, you and your mustang can achieve your highest potential! Look in your own community for help first. Have fun and enjoy the unique spirit and personality of your mustang or burro!

Arkansas

Dawn Rystrom
Northwest Arkansas, southwest Missouri, northeast
   Oklahoma; gentling and training
   (501) 795-2357

Arizona

Johnnie Forquer
Phoenix, Arizona; gentling
   (602) 841-7182; email: jef3382@yahoo.com

Steve Harris
N.A.M.E.—Native American Mustang Educational Institute
Website: www.cowboyschool.com
Video: "A Touch of Love" (highly recommended for first-
   time adopters)
Gentling, training, clinics
   (520) 639-3089; email: name@wildapache.net

California

Audrey Ainsworth
Hopland, CA; training
   (707) 744-1283

Dave and Ginny Freeman
Artois, CA; gentling horses, training burros
   (530) 934-7658

Julie Hueftle
Lincoln, CA; gentling, training
   (916) 645-3609

Brian and Edona Miller
Lincoln, CA; gentling, training
   (530) 633-4252

Bryan Neubert
Alturas, CA; training, clinics
Video: "Wild Horse Handling" (highly recommended for
   first-time adopters)
   (530) 233-3582

Lesley Neuman
Rescue, CA; gentling, training
Video: "The First Touch: Gentling Your Mustang" (highly
   recommended for first-time adopters)
   (530) 677-9205

Jerry Tindell
Hesperia, CA; training, clinics
   (760) 948-1172 ranch; (760) 947-2042 office
   http://members.aol.com/acowboycop

Phil and Karen West
Bishop, CA; training, clinics, California wild horse and burro
   show; www.qnet.com/~sixwranch/home.htm

Allen Worth
Ft. Bragg, CA; training
   (707) 964-2220

Colorado
Mark Rashid
Estes Park, CO; training, clinics
   www.markrashid.com

Connecticut
Kim Dore
Morris, CT; gentling
   (860) 567-8769

Illinois
Danada Wild Horse Project Center
Wheaton, IL
   (630) 668-6012

Indiana
Sheila Noel and David Campbell
Scottsburg, IN; training
   (812) 752-6904

Massachusetts
Cathy Pettey
Westport, MA; gentling
   (508) 636-6691
   http://hometown.aol.com/cpettey941/mustangs.html

Missouri
Deanna Aikin
Kansas City, MO; gentling, rescue, rehabilitation
   (816) 765-2408

Nevada
Jacquie Hill
Reno, NV area; gentling, boarding
   (775) 677-7087

North Carolina
Jill Whitt
Western NC; training
   (828) 497-4719

Oklahoma
Joyce Turner
Fletcher, OK; gentling, training
   (580) 591-3102

Oregon
John Sharp
Prineville, OR; gentling, training
Video: "Bamboo-pole Gentling Clinic" (highly recommended
   for first-time adopters)
   (541) 447-5496

Greg Schultz
Cottage Grove, OR; gentling advice
   (541) 942-9234

South Carolina
Jim, Gale and Jamie Hicks
Anderson, SC; gentling
   (864) 225-2634

Texas
Brooke Wooten
Austin, TX area; gentling, training
   (512) 856-9051

Wisconsin
Grant and Cindy Hohlstein
Granton, WI; gentling, rescue
   (715) 238-7604

Domestic Spanish Mustangs

Many private ranches breed, raise, train, and sell registered Spanish Mustangs whose ancestors date back to original Spanish and Indian stock. These dedicated folks carry on the tradition of keeping historic bloodlines intact, and might even want to share some stories of Spanish Mustang history with you.

Arizona
Apache Trail Spanish Mustangs and Spanish Mustang Registry (Willcox, AZ): (520) 384-2886
  www.angelfire.com/az/xochitl
Celtic Cross Ranch (Apache Junction, AZ): (602) 671-1664
Desert Rare Breeds (Tucson, AZ): (520) 818-0161
  email: SSchne1068@aol.com (Wilbur-Cruce Spanish Colonial Horse)

Idaho
Pleasant Valley Spanish Mustangs (Naples, ID)
  (208) 267-9109

Indiana
Spanish Mustangs (Henryville, IN): (812) 294-4821

Iowa
Enyol' Farm (Afton, IA): (515) 346-2532
One Sky Ranch (Corning, IA): (515) 322-4802

Minnesota
Dream Quest Stables (Foley, MN): (320) 968-7926
Lonesome Dove Registered Spanish Mustangs (Parker's Prairie, MN): (218) 338-5943
WB Farms (St. Cloud, MN): (320) 363-7320
Zen Cowboys' Spanish Mustangs (Lonsdale, MN)
  (507) 744-2704

Mississippi
The 1-13 Ranch (Houston, MS): (601) 568-2097

Nebraska
Spanish Mustangs (Brule, NE): (308) 287-2521

New Mexico
Monero Mustang Ranch (Lumberton, NM): (505) 759-3861 or (505) 759-1893
  www.geocities.com/moneromustangs
Rancho de Abiquiu (Abiquiu, NM): (505) 685-4369
Wilbur-Cruce Mustang Ranch (Caballo, NM)
  (505) 895-5381

Ohio
Prueter's Peaceful Pastures (Grafton, OH): (440) 926-3135

Oklahoma
Rickman's Spanish Mustangs (Soper, OK): (580) 326-6005
(Preserving the Choctaw Horse, bred by the Choctaw
Indian Nation until 1907)

Oregon
Grey Thunder Ranch Spanish Mustangs (Wallowa, OR): (541)
886-5101; www.barrycox.com

South Dakota
Caballos de Destino Spanish Mustangs (Pringle, SD)
(605) 745-4883
Many Ponies Spanish Mustangs (Belle Fourche, SD)
(605) 892-4743

Texas
The American Indian Horse Registry (Lockhart, TX)
(512) 398-6642
www.indianhorse.com
Anne Dolley Original American Indian Horses (Diana, TX):
(903) 968-2196
Dreams in Color Ranch (Canton, TX): (903) 567-5752
www.freeyellow.com/members2/dreams
Karma Farms Spanish Mustangs (Marshall, TX)
(903) 935-9980
www.etexweb.com/personal/speir
Pelt Pond Farm and Rural Life Museum Spanish Mustangs
(Kountze, TX): (409) 287-3516
Rockin' B Ranch (Mabank, TX): (903) 887-7034
email: lbw@tvec.net
Tejas Mustang and Burro Association (Marshall, TX)
(903) 938-2908
www.horsemassage.com
Wild Star Ranch (Wills Point, TX): (903) 896-4237
www.freeyellow.com/members2/wildstar

Utah
Mountain Home Spanish Mustangs (Mantua, UT)
(801) 723-6579

Virginia
Merrie Mead Spanish Mustangs (Chester, VA)
(804) 748-8701
Reed Creek Spanish Mustangs (Gretna, VA)
(804) 656-8182

Wyoming
Cayuse Ranch (Oshoto, WY): (307) 467-5394

Suggested Reading

*available from www.foresthorse.com
†Suggested training book or video especially recommended for first-time adopters

Amaral, Anthony. *Mustang*. University of Nevada Press, Reno, NV, 1977.

Bear-Step, Shatka, *Painted Ponies*, Bear Step Publications, Scottsdale, AZ, 1973.

Bennett, Deb Ph.D, *Conquerors*, Amigo Publications, Inc., Solvang, CA, 1998.

*Brannaman, Buck. *Groundwork: The First Impression*. Rancho Deluxe Design, Marina Del Rey, CA. 1997. (Buck Brannaman also has two videos, *From the Ground Up* and *Groundwork*; see his website www.brannaman.com)

Dines, Glen. *Indian Pony*. MacMillan, NY, 1963.

*Dorrance, Bill. *True Unity*. Give-It-A-Go Enterprises, Bruneau, ID, 1987.

*Dorrance, Tom, *True Horsemanship Through Feel*, Diamond Lu Productions, Canada, 1999. (Tom Dorrance also has a video, *Greetings!*)

Edwards, Elwyn Hartley, *Horses, an Eye Witness Handbook*, DK Publishing, New York, NY, 1993.

Equine Travelers of America, Inc., *Nationwide Overnight Stabling Directory and Equestrian Vacation Guide*, Arkansas City, KS, 1999. [(316) 442-8131] (includes guided trail rides to see wild horses)

Eustis-Cross, Barbara and Bowker, Nancy, *The Wild Horse: An Adopter's Manual*, Macmillan, New York, NY, 1992.

*Genadek, Dave. *About Saddle Fit* (video). Website: www.aboutthehorse.com

Green, Ben K., *Horse Conformation*, Northland Press, Flagstaff, AZ, 1969.

*†Harris, Steve. *A Touch of Love* (video). Website: www.cowboyschool.com

*†Hunt, Ray, *Think Harmony with Horses*, Give-It-A-Go Books, Bruneau, ID, 1978. (Ray Hunt also has a video, *Colt Starting Clinic*, and website, www.rayhunt.com)

*Jackson, Jaime, *The Natural Horse*, Star Ridge Publishing, Harrison, AZ, 1997.

Kirkpatrick, Jay F. and Francis, Michael H., *Into the Wind—Wild Horses of North America*, Northword Press, Minocqua, WI, 1994.

*†Neubert, Bryan. *Wild Horse Handling* (video). Call (530) 233-3582.

*†Neuman, Lesley. *The First Touch: Gentling Your Mustang* (video). Call (530) 677-9205.

Oelke, Hardy, *Born Survivors on the Eve of Extinction*, Ute Kierdorf Verlag, Wipperfurth, Germany, 1997.

*Rashid, Mark, *A Good Horse is Never a Bad Color*, Johnson Books, Boulder, CO, 1996.

*Rashid, Mark, *Considering the Horse*, Johnson Books, Boulder, CO, 1993.

*Rashid, Mark. *Horses Never Lie: The Heart of Passive Leadership*. Johnson Books, Boulder Co, 2000. (Mark Rashid also has a website: www.markrashid.com)

Roberts, Monty, *Shy Boy*, Harper Collins Publishers, Inc., New York, NY, 1999.

Scanlon, Lawrence, *Wild About Horses*, Harper Collins Publishers, Inc., New York, NY, 1998.

Sellnow, Les, *Understanding the Young Horse*, The Blood-Horse, Inc., Lexington, KY, 1999.

Sharp, John. *Knots, Hitches and Their Uses*.
     (Sharp also has a video, *†*John Sharp's Bamboo Poling Method*; call 541-447-5496)

Simpson, George Gaylord, *Horses*, Oxford University Press, New York, NY, 1951.

Sponenberg, D. Philip, DVM, Ph.D., *Equine Color Genetics*, Iowa State University Press, Ames IA, 1996.

Spragg, Mark, Editor, *Thunder of the Mustangs*, Sierra Club Books/Tehabi Books, 1997.

Tellington-Jones, Linda, *Getting in "Touch"*. Trafalgar Square Publishing, North Pomfret, VT, 1995.

Thomas, Heather Smith, *The Wild Horse Controversy*, A.S. Barnes and Co., Inc., Cranbury, NJ, 1979.

Thomas, Shan. *Myth and Mystery: The Curly Horse in America*. (C.S. Fund, Inc., PO Box 520, Sunman, IN 47041)

Twelveponies, Mary, *There Are No Problem Horses, Only Problem Riders*, Houghton Mifflin Company, Boston, MA, 1982.

Watts, Ron, *The Last of the Wild Horses*, Key Porter Books, Toronto, Canada, 1994.

Woolley, Dale E. *The Damales and the American Curly Horse*. 1993.

Worcester, Don, *The Spanish Mustang*, Texas Western Press, The University of Texas at El Paso, TX, 1986.

Xenophon. *The Art of Horsemanship*. First written in 500 BC, translated by M.H. Morgan, Ph.D. J.A. Allen & Co. Ltd., 1999.

Index

Index

Index

The White Mustang

Wherever thrumming hoofbeats drum
As galloping riders go or come;
Wherever a saddle is still a throne
And dust of hoofs by wind is blown;
Wherever are horsemen, young or old,
The Pacing Mustang's tale is told.

—*Anonymous*

Lisa Dines (shown here with two of her adopted mustangs, Clay (left) and Clippy, at home in Ft. Bragg, CA) has been riding horses since age six, and enjoys trail riding on the beach and through the redwoods. She and another adopter, Kate Brennen, established an internet store — Forest Horse (www.foresthorse.com) — to help adopters find specialized books, videos, and supplies for mustangs. (Lisa's son Joel, age 15, who is seen in the book, also loves the horses but prefers to ride his road bike.)

Ms. Dines has a master's degree in counseling psychology and was the former director of a small non-profit animal rescue and rehabilitation organization in Santa Fe, New Mexico. She has adopted, gentled, and trained four BLM mustangs, and her goal is to see all of the herds across the U.S. She currently lives in California.